The Friends Whose Names I'll Never Know

Todd Culp

McHenry County College

Kendall Hunt
publishing company

Cover photographs by Todd Culp.

Kendall Hunt
p u b l i s h i n g   c o m p a n y

www.kendallhunt.com
Send all inquiries to:
4050 Westmark Drive
Dubuque, IA 52004-1840

Printed in the United States of America
10 9 8 7 6 5 4 3 2

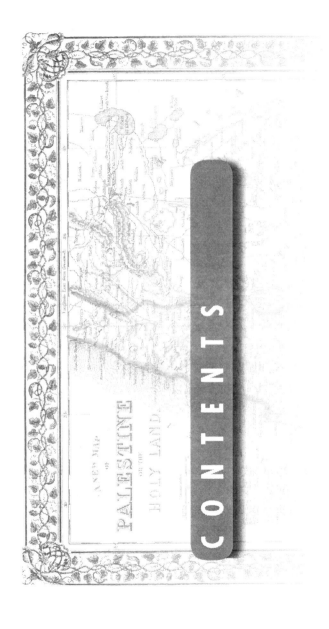

CONTENTS

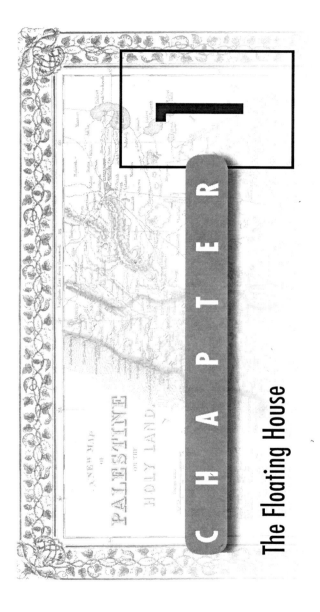

CHAPTER 1

The Floating House

"After they bombed my train station and beheaded those tourists, things calmed down for a few days. But the morning we were supposed to get on our train from Bangkok to travel to the south, I received a call from my contact. He asked if I'd read the morning paper. When I said, no, he commented that there had been a bombing in the town I was traveling to. This time it was a hotel. When he said the name of the hotel, I started laughing, thinking he was joking with me.

"After a minute or two, I realized that I was the only one laughing. He wasn't joking. When I explained that the hotel he was talking about was the hotel I was booked at this evening, he said. 'Oh, well, they only blew up part of the hotel. I'm sure your part's just fine.' So I checked into the hotel later that night."

As I finished the story that I was telling the class about some research I did in southern Thailand during the summer of 2001, a student in the back row asked, "Why do you go to all the ugly places in the world, Dr. Culp?" I've been teaching for about 15 years. After a while, you get good at not being offended by well-intentioned but poorly phrased questions such as this – even those that sum up your life's work as if it was a bad aesthetic choice, like bell bottom pants.

It was actually a good question – one that took a certain amount of courage to even ask. My first reaction was to start laughing. The question was so brazen and yet awkward at the same time. In order to buy myself some time to think, I asked the student, "Why do you see these places as ugly?"

"When you travel to the Middle East or to Southeast Asia, you never talk about seeing the beaches or the mountains. You go to places where bombs go off and people shoot at each other," he said.

"Technically that's true, and while I love beaches and mountains as much as anyone, there are things that are more beautiful."

"Like what?" he asked.

"Being present as heroes are born," I replied. I wasn't sure how to explain this. "Humans are funny creatures. Most creatures on this planet simply try to survive. Much of our behavior is survival based as well, but we also laugh, sing, write poetry, and dance. This is the Midwest, so most of us do it badly, but we do it. We even love, which doesn't always make sense in terms of survival. It would be nice if the list stopped here. But it doesn't. We also plot, scheme, rape, torture, and commit genocide. If you want to understand both sides of humanity, to understand why humans do what they do, the best place to study this is in the zones of conflict. Obviously in zones of conflict, you will see the worst side of human nature, but ironically, it's also where you will see the best.

"Heroes emerge from the ashes watered by the blood of others. Pressure affects people differently. Some rise to the occasion. Some sink beneath its depths. Further, the conflict itself acts like a magnet drawing others from abroad into the cauldron to see if they will sink or rise. Although entering this cauldron, you will undoubtedly witness horrific things you would expunge from your memory if you could; the cauldron is also the heart of beauty. Humans engage in selfless acts that boggle the mind. A man whose entire life and that of his family had been destroyed by the Israelis, makes it his life's work to reach out and call them brothers. A woman whose son was killed by a Palestinian sniper, reaches out to the sniper's mother in a gesture of forgiveness and reconciliation. Soldiers, both Israeli and Palestinian, meet together to discuss the atrocities they have personally committed against one another and ask for the unthinkable: forgiveness, and perhaps, even friendship. These things make something as grand as a mountain seem rather small."

I don't pretend to understand these people fully — these peacemakers (for lack of a better, less clichéd term). I have spent the majority of my academic life trying to understand a very different type of people. I've always been fascinated by the question of why people are willing to fight, kill, or die for their principles. As a result, I began my career studying the combatants, not the peacemakers. I've conducted interviews with groups such as Hamas and Islamic Jihad in the West Bank. I've spent time talking to people in Southeast Asia in the midst of a conflict marked by the targeted killings of priests and teachers. Not only are the targets of these killings a testament to the nature of the conflict, but let's not forget that *I am a teacher*. I tried not to take it personally. I've spent the afternoon sipping tea on the front porch of a man who was educated, eloquent, and heartbroken. He was also a member of an organization whose members were comfortable with the idea of strapping a bomb to one's chest and walking into a crowded mall. I've spoken with Israeli soldiers who are comfortable with the concept that there is no such thing as civilians. Women, children, and the elderly are all fair game.

But these peacemakers about whom I write this time, are difficult to understand. They are easy to admire but hard to figure. Many of them are perfectly willing to fight and die but not to kill. Others are willing to forgive the unforgivable. But to look at the combatants and the peacemakers as two fully distinct groups, creates a false dichotomy and tempts us to hubris. It's easy to label the combatants as villains and the peacemakers as heroes and thus identify ourselves with the heroes. This vastly oversimplifies the motivations of the combatants and does not give nearly enough credit to the peacemakers.

Because at the end of the day, as much as we admire the peacemakers, we share more in common with the combatants than we would like to admit. I am fascinated with these peacemakers precisely because I'm not sure that I could ever be one. I've used their tactics before I ever knew they were tactics. It was simply the right thing to do at the time. I've stood between the soldier's guns and their intended targets. I've played the fool in order to distract soldiers taking out their bad mood on an unlucky fruit vendor. So yes, I've dabbled in what they do. But the people about whom I write do this *every day*, day in and day out. Many of them have suffered losses that I cannot fathom, and still they rise to the occasion. Too many of them have lost children in this conflict, and still they reach across the battle lines to grasp the hand of an enemy in the solidarity of pain.

I speak as a man who has three little girls around whom not only does the world revolve, but the universe as well. I cannot fathom – I do not allow myself to fathom – the places that I would go or the things that I would do, should even one of them be harmed in any way. I feel a rage of biblical proportion when someone so much as hurts their feelings. It is one thing for me to put myself in harm's way to protect someone whom I believe is being unfairly treated, but to love an enemy who has taken the dearest thing in my life away from me, is beyond my capacity to imagine. If we're truly honest with ourselves, we may have more in common with the combatants I studied than with the peacemakers.

✖ THE FLOATING HOUSE ✖

Two men stood underneath the floating house. It's not unusual that the two men were standing on the land. The land had been in their families for many generations. Even the Israeli Supreme Court had admitted, in a surprising decision a few months earlier, that the land was theirs. It may seem strange that the Supreme Court needed to tell these men that their land was indeed *their* land, but this is the West Bank, and they are Palestinians, so tragically, it's not uncommon for their land to be taken from them. For nearly three years, these men and the people of the village had been protesting the decision of the Israeli military to build a wall separating them from their farmland, their livelihood. To use the word, wall, is insufficient. In the media back here in the United States, it's often referred to as a security fence. And indeed, there are sections of the wall that are merely a fence, but the overwhelming majority that I've seen in the West Bank does not fit the standard definition of *fence*. Instead, it is a concrete wall twice the height of the Berlin Wall with 30-foot gun towers for observation. To describe it as intimidating would be a criminal understatement.

So as I stated earlier, it's understandable why these two men would be standing on their land, but why would anyone stand underneath the floating house, especially when it's not theirs? As we take a closer look, the picture becomes more chaotic. The house was suspended from a crane, and there was a mob of men shouting, "Crush them! Crush them!" Neither the mob nor the floating house had a legal right to be on the land. They were trespassers. And yet, when you have power on your side, law can seem to be a trivial matter. The two men stood calmly under the dangling house as the mob called for them to be crushed. The crane operator revved the engine in an attempt to intimidate them. The men refused to move. The mob began to yell and scream at the two men. They didn't flinch. At this point begins a macabre and darkly humorous dance as the crane operator attempted to swing the house away from the men and drop it fully intact onto the ground. The two men refused to give the mob this easy victory. As the house moved, they moved. To the left. Back to the right. Again and again. The mob screamed insults and threats, as the men did this deadly Charleston two-step with the crane and the dangling house. When the crane operator stopped swinging the house, the dance ended, and any trace of humor – even the darkest kind – evaporated.

The mob's mood went from dark to pitch black. You could hear glass breaking as bottles and rocks were thrown at the men standing beneath the floating house. Then a member of the mob walked up to one of the men under the house and punched him square in the face. The punch was strong enough to spin him around. Remarkably, he slowly turned back around and stood his ground. He did not retaliate. He did not utter a single aggressive word. He simply said, "We wish to live in peace. If you wish to hit me, then hit me. If you wish to kill me, then kill me. But you have no legal right to be on this land" (Rahma). The man struck him again. Again he slowly turned around and confronted the man with words, not violence. "Hit me again if you must." And again the man struck him. As he turned around this time he said, "Hit me again. You're on camera" (Rahma).

While I would love to know what went through the man's mind as he heard these words, because it's always nice to see a bully flinch, these unfortunate words sent part of the mob running up the hill to assault the cameraman. He was beaten by the mob, and his camera smashed. However, in three years of nonviolent protests, taking beatings every week, these people have learned a few things. The cameraman managed to get the tape out of the camera and hide it as the mob ran at him. Think about that for a moment. He could've just run and possibly gotten away, but he chose to take the beating because the tape was that important. The tape showed the brutality that he and his people regularly face. You can now see the tape on the Internet.

Unfortunately, the tape shows only the beginning of this incident and some of the beating. This entire series of beatings will last approximately 45 minutes total. Predictably, after the camera's accusing eye was removed, the violence spiraled upward. The mob returned its focus to the two men standing firm under the floating house. About 20 members of the mob converged on the two men, and a much more serious beating commenced. The men were beaten to the ground, where they were kicked and stomped on repeatedly until they started to lose consciousness. They might have never regained consciousness had they not told the mob that the police had been called and were on their way. The police *had* been called, but they didn't show up for quite some time. However, the perception that the police were on the way gave a new sense of urgency to this illegal mob. As a result, they dragged the semi-conscious bodies of the two men out from under the floating house, allowing the crane operator to successfully put it on the ground that did not belong to them.

The mob packed to leave before the police showed up, as did the crane operator. And then something truly amazing happened. The two men, regaining consciousness from their beating, did the unthinkable. Unable to walk, they slowly crawled over and put their bodies in front of the wheels of the crane. Why would someone do this? They wanted to preserve as much evidence of this crime as possible for the police, when they finally did show up. These men believed so deeply in the rule of law – even the Israeli law that had harmed them so many times in the past – that they were willing to put their bodies underneath the wheels of the crane. I know very few people, even in well-established democracies, who believe in the rule of law that much. This is not the picture that we normally see of Palestinians on the news in America. Yet these people and hundreds of others in villages across the West Bank, have been exercising their rights to free speech and free assembly every week for years.

I wish the story had a happy ending. The mob then circled the crane and tried to pull the men's bodies out from underneath it. The men positioned themselves far enough underneath the crane that this was impossible. So the mob began to throw stones at the men's faces. This went on for some time. The Israeli soldiers who guarded the area looked on. Their main focus was to prevent the villagers from coming to the aid of the two men being stoned. From the crowd of villagers, someone yelled that the police were coming. The mob decided it was better to leave their bloody work unfinished. The crane operator jumped off the crane and decided to leave on foot, since his machine was paralyzed by the bodies of the two men. At this point, the two men summoned up all the strength they had left and ran after the crane operator, yelling for the police to arrest him, still placing their faith in the rule of law. But it was, indeed, all of their strength. They fainted from the pain and exertion. As they fell to the ground, the bloody ground that had been their father's father's land for as long as they could remember, a few remaining members of the mob returned for one last attempt to finish the men. The police prevented this. Neither the crane operator nor the mob was arrested.

A member of Peace Now, an Israeli peace activist group, arrived and helped get the men to the hospital. Twenty minutes later, an ambulance showed up. They drove a few miles to the Israeli military checkpoint between them and the next town. They were then forced to wait for 30 minutes at the checkpoint before being allowed through to the hospital. Once again, due to the miracle of modern Internet technology, you can now see the photos taken of these men as they were wheeled into the hospital. They are not pretty.

As I spoke to one of the two men a few weeks later, he spoke of the event as a victory. Let that word resonate in your head for a moment: a victory. How wretched does life have to be for a nightmarish scene such as this, to be a victory? The fact I could even ask such a question illustrates that I've grown up in an environment where rule of law usually wins the day. This man has not. This incident was a victory because two days later, the mobile homes were removed by the police. Many times, this does not happen. Many times, the mob wins. This is how many of the illegal Israeli settlements throughout the West Bank have begun.

This incident was a victory because this man and his people were able to hold onto the Supreme Court decision that said their land was indeed their land. Not that the military has followed the Supreme Court decision and removed the wall illegally built on their land; it hasn't. But they still have hope. This is a land where that's not only something, *that's everything*. In a later chapter, I'll discuss Father Chacour, the Palestinian Christian Archbishop of Galilee. To this day, 60 years later, he and his people cannot return to their village, which was taken from them by the Israeli Military in 1948, and they are actually citizens of Israel. The Palestinians of the West Bank don't have the luxury of that type of citizenship. Their villages and cities are being walled in, creating open-air prisons.

On my last trip to the Middle East in 2008, I was struck by what a friend of mine, who is an expert on refugees, had to say. He was interviewing Palestinian refugees in Lebanon. He described their conditions as horrific. This statement has a lot of weight coming from a man who was in charge of a football stadium full of refugees during the Rwandan massacre. These Palestinian refugees had been living under these conditions for generations. When my friend asked whether they would prefer to remain there or to move back to the West Bank if that were an option, their response shocked me. They preferred to stay where they were. When he asked why, they said, "I may be poor but least free." Those words rang in my ears, as I saw village after village cut off from each other and the rest of the world, by walls and checkpoints. Yet, I said this man and the people of his village still have hope. I don't have the words to describe how remarkable that is to me.

Who is this man, willing to be crushed for his principles and the future of his people? He is a man who has led peaceful, nonviolent protests against the Israeli military on his land for three years. He shows up every week without fail. He is amazing in one sense, but in another, he is simply one example of the many villagers throughout the West Bank, who come out every week and do the same thing. He is a hard man to interview. Ten days after his beating delayed our first interview, he was shot in the head by a steel bullet with a rubber coating at the weekly protests. This delayed our interview yet again.

He has been hospitalized 20 to 30 times over the last three years in these peaceful, nonviolent protests. This is why I can truly only use the words, *peaceful* and *nonviolent*, when referring to the protesters. The Israeli soldiers who come out to meet the protesters every week regularly employ violence against them. I read injury reports from the protests every week. I cannot remember a week where there were not substantial casualties.

According to an Israeli human rights organization, between September of 2000 and March of 2008, there have been 4,719 Palestinians killed by the Israelis in the West Bank and Gaza ("Trigger-Happy"). Between September of 2000 and February of 2008, there have been 32,213 injuries: 7,049 of those injuries were due to rubber/plastic bullets, and 6,683 were caused by tear gas (Palestine Red Crescent Society Website, 2008). Beyond the injuries, the rubber bullets and the tear gas, are all too often, lethal. And yet this is a man who teaches his people about the ideas of Mahatma Gandhi and Martin Luther King. It's hard to describe what a tear gas canister can do to the human body. I've seen the after-effects where it not only burned through the flesh, but through the muscle tissue. When rubber bullets strike the victim in the head, it's often fatal.

This is Abdullah Abu Rahma. He's a teacher and he has two daughters that are five and three. I am a teacher. My two older daughters are five and three. I am a year older than Abdullah, and the third addition to my family is a baby girl named Rebekkah. We joked that since we seem to be following the same pattern, he would probably have a baby girl soon, too. I learned a long time ago to make jokes as a way of dealing with painful situations. However, this struck a bit too close to home.

Each time I travel to the Middle East, my family and friends worry about my safety, knowing that the places I go are not always stable. For my part, there is always a struggle between the importance of telling these stories of unknown heroes and the importance of being a good father. I can't even pretend to imagine the internal struggle he faces every week, as he stands for his people amidst a hail of steel bullets with rubber coatings and tear gas, all too often followed by beatings. And yet as we spoke, he never mentioned this. What he did want to convey was a message of peace for both Palestinians and Israelis.

To the Israelis, he said, "We are not against you, not even the soldiers. We simply need our land. We only want peace for us and our children. We are not terrorists. We only want to live on our land." To the Palestinians, he said, "We cannot succeed by the violent method." This is a man who could lead the violent resistance if he chose to. He commands respect from both Palestinians and Israelis. In 2005, Abdullah was arrested on false charges and imprisoned for several weeks. In response, hundreds of demonstrators showed up in T-shirts with the words, "I am Abdullah Abu Rahma" written across the chest. The phrase was written in Hebrew, English, Arabic, Russian, French, and Spanish. The crowd of demonstrators included over 80 Israelis. This is a man to be reckoned with.

Sometimes when I'm talking to my students, I ask them to free-associate with the word *Palestinian*. Their response is typical of most Americans that I encounter. The words, terrorist or suicide bomber, are the most common answers. This should give us pause. In the last couple of years, there have been three suicide bombings in Israel. These are indeed horrible events and should be remembered. However, these village protests against the Israeli military building the wall on their land, have been going on every week during this same time period. The protests are peaceful and nonviolent. The number of people involved in each of these peaceful, nonviolent protests ranges from dozens to hundreds. The protests happen at many different sites all across the West Bank simultaneously. So, each week, we are conservatively looking at several hundred people engaging in peaceful, nonviolent resistance to the taking of their land. Multiply that by fifty-two weeks in a year over several years, and you have tens of thousands of incidents of people, choosing the nonviolent path in the face of horrible circumstances. So remind me again, why the automatic association we make with Palestinians is that of the suicide bomber?

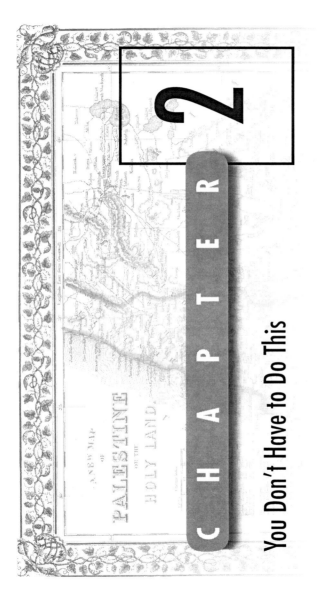

CHAPTER 2

You Don't Have to Do This

As they moved us to the side of the small building, out of sight of the others, and the soldiers leveled their guns towards us, the student to my right said, "You don't have to do this."

"Yeah. Yeah, I think I do," I replied.

"They will shoot you. You understand that, right?" he said.

"Yes. I'm clear on that point, but thanks for bringing it up. I feel *much better* about the decision now that you brought up the possibility of death," I replied.

This rather awkward conversation was taking place at an Israeli checkpoint. I wasn't really supposed to be there. When I woke up that morning, I intended to go to Ramallah to do research. As I was getting ready to leave, a friend came by my room and asked if I was going on the trip to Haifa.

"No," I replied.

"Come on," he said. "You haven't left Birzeit in a month."

"I go to Ramallah all the time."

"That doesn't count. Come on, there's an open seat on the bus. Thomas isn't going."

We rolled down the street in an old bus that reminded me of the one that took me to school when I was a kid. It even had safety windows that didn't open all the way. There may have even been those black lines drawn by permanent marker on the window frame, showing just how far the window was supposed to come down, but I don't remember. We eventually arrived at an Israeli checkpoint at the Green Line. I asked Marcus, who was sitting next to me, if everyone on the bus had clearance to cross the Green Line. He knew exactly what I meant. There were approximately 15 internationals on the bus who had gathered for this trip, but there were also two Palestinian students from Birzeit University. The internationals probably wouldn't have a serious problem at the checkpoint – just the standard hassle. The two Palestinian students, however, were guaranteed a hard time, even if they did have clearance to leave their zone in the West Bank. Further, we had all heard the stories recently of Palestinians who had been stopped at a checkpoint and then never heard from again.

"They should be fine," Marcus said. "They submitted their paperwork nine months ago for this trip and have been approved."

I really didn't know many of the people on the bus. I was simply looking forward to sitting on a beach in Haifa. I watched as the Israeli soldier's automatic rifles bounced semi-rhythmically against the seats of the bus as they walked towards us, checking passports. When they arrived at the seat with the two Palestinians sitting in it, they asked for paperwork. Before the Palestinian students could produce their approval notice, they were dragged off the bus at gunpoint. The driver of the bus was told to drive on. He engaged the clutch and started to close the doors.

This really shouldn't have shocked me. I had been living in the West Bank for a while now. I had been witness to some horrible things. At that point, it was simply inconceivable to me that this Palestinian bus driver was about to leave two Palestinian kids at a checkpoint alone, knowing full well that their story could end tragically. This event took place almost 15 years ago, during the first Intifada, and I've learned a few things since then. Without fully knowing the man's situation, I really wasn't in a position to judge him. But this was 15 years ago, and I wasn't nearly as enlightened as I am now. I also had more hair. I ran toward the front of the bus yelling for the driver to stop.

"They say go. I go," was his response to my yells.

"Then open the door," I replied.

I jumped off the bus and turned around in time to see the bus driver slowly shaking his head. "Your choice. Young, brave, *and* stupid," he muttered under his breath.

I asked the Israeli soldiers why the two students were being detained. The first soldier said that no Palestinians were allowed to leave the West Bank today. I then explained that the students had applied for written permission from the Israeli government nine months in advance and had received it. He responded that legal rights were only for humans, and Palestinians were just animals. I asked when he was planning to release these students to go home. He laughed and said, "Who said we're going to release them?"

This conversation transpired in only a few minutes, so fortunately the bus driver had not left yet. In a short period of time, I had persuaded all the other internationals on the bus to come out and stand in the middle of the checkpoint with me. This made it nearly impossible for the bus driver to leave. It also made it very difficult for traffic to move through the checkpoint. I again approached Israeli soldiers. This time, I purposely avoided the soldier that I had first talked to, hoping to find a more reasonable person to discuss the problem with instead. As I approached a different soldier, he initially seemed angry and requested that I move my friends away from the checkpoint. I responded that I'd love to move them out of the checkpoint and go sit on a beach in Haifa, but that I couldn't, in good conscience, leave two members of our group behind.

"They have proper papers. What else is necessary for them to get back on the bus?" I asked.

"They're not going to get back on the bus with you," he said.

"Then we have a problem because I don't feel safe leaving them behind."

"I'm not going to hurt them."

"I'm not really worried about you. It's your friend over there that concerns me."

"He's not my friend."

"Can you guarantee their safety?"

"No."

"Then we have a problem," I said again.

Even though I hadn't persuaded the soldier to let the students get back on the bus, he seemed like a reasonable person. I had some hope that we could eventually work this out.

At this point, a soldier, more angry than the first, walked into the crowd of people that I had just asked to get off the bus with me. He was pointing his automatic rifle about the face level at the people in the crowd and continuously chambering it. This had the desired effect of frightening the people in the crowd. I took a few steps over to where he was and asked him to please stop. I explained he was scaring people. At this point, he turned the rifle towards me and began chambering it again and again. Unfortunately, this struck me as oddly amusing. All I could think was that this gesture, clearly intended to intimidate, was simply demonstrating over and over again that his gun was empty. Apparently this thought showed up on my face. I know I didn't laugh, but one can't know exactly what one's face looks like in a situation like this. I assume I must've had a slight (very unintentional) smile on my face because something set him off. He inserted a full clip into his rifle and began aggressively shoving me backwards while yelling in Hebrew. At some point, I decided to stop allowing him to shove me and we reached an impasse. Tensions rose quickly. The more reasonable soldier approached and told the other soldier to calm down. This seemed to anger him even more, and he began moving the barrel closer to my face. I turned to the more reasonable soldier and said, "You are just about to have an international incident where I am shot in front of 15 witnesses from 15 different nations. Is that what you want?" In reality, that was probably an exaggeration. I think there were only about eight countries represented there, but my continual, involuntary, and rather close inspection of the man's rifle barrel, made it difficult for me to count accurately.

After a heated exchange in Hebrew, of which I understood very little, the angry soldier pulled his gun away from my forehead and stalked away. The more reasonable soldier turned to me and said, "You need to move these people out of this checkpoint so the traffic can move through."

"I'd be happy to move them all over to the side of the road as long as you talk to your commander about getting clearance for these two Palestinian students. They have the proper paperwork. They've done nothing wrong," I responded.

"You can move all the internationals to the side of the road, but the two Palestinians must stay here behind the checkpoint gate," he said.

"We wouldn't be able to see them if we're way over there and they're behind the gate," I replied.

"That's the only option," he retorted. His tone was becoming angry.

"Can I have someone from my group stand with them to make sure that nothing happens to them?" I asked.

"Fine. But only one of you," he said as he walked away.

As I turned towards my group, they were all looking at me with the same expression. The decision was rather obvious. So, after I moved the group to the side of the road, the soldiers escorted the two students and myself back behind the gate out of view of the others. At this stage, they pointed the guns directly at us.

The student to my right said, "You don't have to do this."

"Yeah. Yeah, I think I do," I replied.

"They will shoot you. You understand that, right?" he said.

"Yes. I'm clear on that point, but thanks for bringing it up. I feel *much better* about the decision now that you brought up the possibility of death," I replied.

My standard response to stress comes in the form of attempts at humor or sarcasm – often unsuccessful and in this case, rather desperate – but humor, nonetheless.

"You don't have to …" he started to say again when I cut him off. "Can we just not talk for a moment? I need to think."

As my mind raced through all the possible scenarios and what I could possibly say or do, time marched on. After the first few minutes had passed, and it was clear they weren't intending on shooting us any time soon, my mind began to wander. How the hell did I get into this situation? Not just this checkpoint, but this country? This conflict? My high school guidance counselor had told me that I shouldn't bother going to college because I wasn't really college material. While the comment irritated me at the time, I couldn't help but notice that if I had followed his advice, it was very likely that I would not be in a situation where I was passing time by observing that the soldier on the left hadn't cleaned the barrel of his rifle quite as judiciously as had the soldier on the right.

Although many of my friends have since told me I would be perfectly justified sending a copy of my PhD in the mail to my high school guidance counselor, he wasn't completely wrong. Based upon both my school records and my police record, I wasn't exactly the poster boy for college recruiters. I was reasonably intelligent and creative, but that creativity more often than not brought trouble, not accolades. In fact, the principal at my high school graduation used stories of my exploits as a cautionary tale as he gave his speech. He also tossed an orange water balloon off the stage near the seated students to illustrate why one should never trust a student like me. My parents were so proud.

Beyond my misspent creativity, I was not from the prototypical college family. I'm the last of seven kids, most of whom either never went to college or didn't finish. I want to be clear, this is not a criticism of my family. In my family culture, going to college was simply one option among many, once you graduated from high school. It was not even the most desired option. Working hard and raising a family was what life was about. College was simply a means to an end and was to be used only if necessary.

The small blue-collar town that I grew up in had a couple of factories to choose from. Nearly all of my friends' and classmates' parents worked at one or both of these factories. As a result, many of us were encouraged not to go to college. The factories and the military were popular options. Grad school and a PhD program were not.

Ironically, or perhaps predictably if you know me, it was my high school counselor's advice that sent me in the direction of college and my church's dogmatic support of Israel that sent me to the Middle East. I grew up in a religious tradition that believed Israel to be a fulfillment of prophecy, which could therefore do no wrong. Those that blessed Israel would be blessed. Those that cursed Israel would be cursed. This led to rather logical conclusions. If God was on Israel's side, that meant they were 100% right. If Israel was 100% right, that meant the Palestinians were not.

As I worked my way through college, I often held two or three jobs at the same time. Between all these jobs and a full-time college schedule, I had the opportunity to meet many different types of people. The image of one side being completely right or completely wrong began to crumble. In school, I was slowly learning the language and the methods of an academic. However, as I read the literature on the Palestinian-Israeli conflict, I found it to be rather polarized. It was hard to find voices in the middle. As a result, I looked back to my working-class roots for an answer. My father had always taught me that, if you want to know what's really going on in a situation, you need to go to the people involved and ask them. I don't believe he ever intended this advice to become a justification for his youngest son to take his first trip outside the country to land in the middle of a revolution. I have to admit, as the father of three young children myself now, this part of the story is not as funny as it used to be.

Scraping together the money for a plane ticket to the Middle East turned out to be harder than I thought. As a result, I took the cheapest route available. Not one of my wisest decisions. The airline, based in Romania, decided to take quite a few scheduled stops in Europe and at least one unscheduled stop somewhere near the Yugoslav-Romanian border, on its way to the Middle East. A woman began to read the announcements over the microphone as we flew out of Chicago, stating them first in Romanian and then in English. However, as her eyes drifted over the crowd, she realized there was really only one English speaker on the plane. With this realization, she dispensed with English translation altogether. Because of this, I was never really clear why we made the unscheduled stop at the small airport in the middle of nowhere.

I asked the Romanian man seated next to me why the plane was descending when I couldn't see the city or an airport. He said that it was very small. This turned out to be very true. It's the only time I've landed at an airport that was so small, you can only see the runway after you've landed on it. As we landed, I realized that part of the runway had been obscured by camouflage netting. Why camouflage netting, you might ask? Well, it's to cover up the Mig fighter jets, of course. I didn't have long to look at the Mig fighter jets because as the plane rolled to a stop, it was met by a tank.

As the tank approached the plane, I asked the Romanian gentlemen seated next to me if he thought I could get away with taking a picture of the tank through the plane window. Although his English was not great, he managed to communicate rather effectively. His exact words were, "Maybe you do? Maybe they…" At this, he put his hands out in front of him and locked his wrists together like they were handcuffed. He said this with such comic indifference and a shrug of the shoulders, that it was clear it would not upset him terribly if they did arrest me. I guess the empty seat would have provided a bit more legroom. It must be said that this is a man who had fled Romania with part of his family during the Chauchescu Period and was only now returning for the rest of his children and his wife. I dropped the camera back into my bag.

Several men with large guns, small berets, and no sense humor boarded the plane. Several people were taken off the plane, and in no time we were back in the air, minus a few passengers. I always assumed that they were coming back. I was in my early 20s and still a bit naïve about things like this. I still wonder what happened to them. Eventually, after an eight-hour layover in Bucharest involving more men with large guns, small berets, and no sense humor, I made it to the Middle East.

The gun barrels were directed away from us as the more reasonable soldier returned to talk to me. He'd been gone for what seemed like an eternity. It was difficult to tell how long it actually was. Time has a way of distorting itself when your mortality is in question. Later, I found out that the entire incident had taken a couple of hours. This was unusual at the time for internationals traveling in Israel, but it was and still is simply daily life for the Palestinians. Ultimately, we were allowed to get back on the bus with the two Palestinian students. Before boarding the bus, I stopped to speak to the more reasonable soldier one last time.

"How do you do this, day in and day out? It must be difficult for someone like you," I said.

"What exactly do you mean by someone like me?" he asked.

"You seem like a reasonable man. I don't think you view the Palestinians as animals, whereas some of your comrades clearly do. Brutal things happen at checkpoints like this. That's got to be difficult for you," I responded. I have never forgotten his reply. He said, "Yes. Brutal things do happen here. But this is not who I am. This is simply something I'm required to do for a few years. When I'm done with my service, I will move far away from here and never think again on what was done in this place." I was struck by both the honest and delusional character of the statement. He believed and clearly hoped that he could erase these horrible memories over time. I suddenly felt sorry for the man.

"I've seen many things here that will be stuck in my head for the rest of my life, whether I want them to or not," I said. "Maybe you're different. I doubt it. But for your sake, I hope so." After I said this to the soldier, he simply shook his head and looked at the ground. A few minutes later, I was on the bus headed for Haifa.

This story yet again demonstrates that not all Israelis and Palestinians view each other in the same way. One of the soldiers clearly viewed Palestinians as less than animals. The other soldier viewed them quite differently. Two soldiers, both Israeli, both working the same checkpoint with two very different perspectives. What accounts for this? I am frequently told by people that this is a religious conflict, and they hate each other based upon their religions. Yet I don't believe I've ever witnessed an intense theological debate between Israelis and Palestinians that involved guns. This is one of those myths that we hold on to concerning this conflict because we think it helps us to understand it. It gives us something to say when we discuss this complex conflict. Unfortunately, it ultimately obfuscates much more than it illuminates. I will discuss why this is a myth in more detail in the next chapter.

Going back to the original question, it's hard to believe that it was simply religion that caused one of the soldiers to hate Palestinians, but not the other. Neither of the men was that religious. I believe it goes deeper than that. There are many myths about this conflict that I will discuss in this book. Generally, they are dangerous oversimplifications with hardly a grain of truth to be found in them. They are just our stock answers when this topic comes up at the dinner party, the bar, the water cooler, and more disturbingly, at the church. If we need an oversimplification to explain this conflict, then I recommend this one: It's about fear. It's about saying to yourself that *this will never* happen again to my child, my mother, my wife. I've spoken to so many people on both sides of this conflict, that had been victimized by the other and have sworn it will never happen again. Whatever it takes, it won't happen again. When they say, "whatever it takes," they mean it in a way that most of us cannot comprehend. I pray that we never can.

However, one does not have to be a direct victim of violence to be guided by a sense of victimhood. In talking to these soldiers, I found that neither one of them had had a friend or family member harmed in the conflict. Yet one of them had clearly been raised in an environment of fear that they would become victims again, as Jews in the past so often have been. An Israeli scholar, Daniel Bar-Tal states that the Israelis have often used the Holocaust to legitimize excessive security measures, and to continually remind the world about Jewish victimhood through the ages. The excessive military methods used in dealing with their perception of a threat, are also a demonstration to the world that they will never be victims again (Bar-Tal and Dikla). This sets in motion a deadly progression. John Mack, a scholar on conflict resolution, states that it is "difficult in the face of civilized codes of morality to commit mass murder against another people unless that people [is] first deprived of their claim to consideration as human beings" (125). Ervin Staub says that "feelings of responsibility are subverted by excluding certain people from the realm of humanity or defining them as dangerous to one's self and one's way of life and values... a complete reversal of morality may occur, so that murder becomes a service to humanity" (83). This psychological process provides the mechanism for a soldier, such as the one who viewed Palestinians as animals, to do anything he wants to a Palestinian at his checkpoint and view himself as not only justified, but even virtuous.

The good news is that many Israelis have transcended this fear and this sense of victimhood. I will discuss several of them in this book. Palestinians as well, are vulnerable to this cycle of fear and victimhood. I have met very few Palestinians that don't carry the physical scars of this conflict on their bodies or have family members who do. This is what's so remarkable about the people I discuss in this book. They have risen above this deadly cycle. There are so many more that I haven't included as well. These people, both Palestinian and Israeli, are the foundation of any future peace in this region. Yet we seldom hear about them.

Although the story that I tell in this chapter happened years ago, the situation with checkpoints has only grown progressively worse with the passage of time. According to the Israeli group Peace Now, there are nearly 600 checkpoints in the West Bank alone (Fisher-Ilan). This, in a chunk of land that is only about 30 miles wide and about 90 miles long. The majority of these checkpoints do not restrict Palestinian movement from the West Bank into Israel. Most of the checkpoints restrict Palestinian movement from one place inside the West Bank to another place inside the West Bank. Hence, most Palestinians doubt that the checkpoints are really there for security reasons. The frequent humiliations and casualties as a result of the checkpoints, fuel this opinion amongst Palestinians. Fifty-three Palestinians have died since the end of 2000 because soldiers detained them at checkpoints when they needed medical attention ("Trigger-Happy"). During the same time period, 69 women have been forced to give birth at a checkpoint. The result was that 35 of the babies and five of the mothers died. Brain damage resulted in some of the babies who survived ("Discriminatory Policies against Palestinians in East J'lem").

How did this conflict get to the point where both Palestinians and Israelis justifiably view themselves as the victim and, as a result, feel justified in doing horrible things to one another? There are many well-written histories of this very complex conflict. I am not attempting that Herculean task here, but the following chapter will discuss some of the main events in that history. To avoid boring the reader with a history full of names, dates, and wars, I will cover the history through the eyes of remarkable peacemakers who lived through many of the pivotal events in the history of the conflict.

CHAPTER 3

"I Don't Know Why the Children Still Smile"

"I cannot answer your question. I don't know why the children still smile" (Chacour). His face was tired and worn but still patient. It reminded me of the way he had once described his own father's face. He had graciously agreed to an interview with me even though I'm pretty sure, judging from his expression, he wasn't informed that my interview was scheduled for this moment in time. He's a very busy and important man, but at the same time, he's still a boy from Galilee. As I looked into this older man's eyes, I could still see a bit of the boy. The following stories are drawn from my conversations with Arch Bishop Chacour, as well as his own autobiographical work (Chacour; Chacour and Weaver).

✂ THE GALILEAN HILLS ✂

He was a curious boy, but more curious than normal today, as he roamed the hills of Galilee. His brother had told him that his father was going to buy lamb. This meant a celebration. Yet no holidays were imminent. Yes, he was very curious. He ran through the streets of the village looking for his father. Someone suggested he might've gone to the Jewish village nearby. His father traded with the men from this village regularly. He remembered their Jewish neighbors arriving at their home and the smell of deep, rich coffee, as his father made the traditional cup of friendship. He also remembered with excitement, the large black car that one of the men arrived in. He'd never seen a car before. This was 1947.

His father returned with a young lamb and weary feet. He was a calm and peaceful man who radiated those qualities. Yet there was an unmistakably deep sadness in his eyes. As the children gathered around, he began explaining that something horrible had happened. In the faraway land of Europe, an evil man had come to power and done unspeakable things to the Jewish people. The stories chilled the young boy to his very center. His father assured them that Hitler was now gone, but their Jewish brothers were troubled that they could not return to their homes in Europe. Europe was not quick to embrace the return of Jews to their former homes (Bankier), and would stay in their home for a few days. The boy observed the range of emotions revealed on the faces of his older siblings, as his father told him that the men carried machine guns, but they didn't kill.

The boy's gentle father saw that it was time to change the subject. He said the children would be able to sleep under the stars on the roof. He knew that this would excite the children. It would also make more room for the soldiers. Further, he would prepare a lamb for the feast. They would honor their new guests with a feast normally saved only for holidays.

The Jewish soldiers arrived, but they were not like the boy's Jewish neighbors with whom they'd shared coffee so many times. They carried guns and spoke little. The feast did not feel like a celebration. They even carried their guns to the dinner table. The boy rarely saw guns in his village. There were only two or three rusty old rifles in the entire village saved to scare the wolves away from the sheep.

After a week of sleeping on the roof, the experience lost some of its excitement. The boy wondered when the soldiers would leave. The next day, the men of the village were called to a meeting with the soldiers. The soldiers' commander told the men of the village that it was in danger. The men remembered back in the 1930s, when Jewish paramilitary soldiers like these had attacked the British troops, resulting in violent battles. The commander said that it would be best if the people left the village for a few days. The soldiers could defend it. This made the men of the village uneasy, but they didn't want their families caught in the midst of a gun battle. So they gathered their families and agreed to leave for a few days. Since they would only be there for a short time, the villagers moved to the shelter of the olive groves. After nightfall, the weather turned cold, and the rain came. A few days turned into weeks.

It was particularly hard on the elderly of the village. The soldiers had told them to travel light. This left them with little between them and the elements. Finally, the elders of the village decided to risk going back to talk to the soldiers. They had not seen or heard any evidence of the battle. Perhaps the trouble had passed. As they walked slowly into the village, they were stunned. No battle had taken place but the village had indeed been violated. Doors were kicked in. Dishes and furniture were smashed. Drapes were shredded. As the realization began to sink in, it was confirmed as armed soldiers told them to get out. They had no business here anymore.

Their trust and hospitality had been returned with betrayal. They couldn't understand how this could be happening. The families that made up this village had been living on this land and farming these fields for more generations than anyone could remember. In this way, they were like all the other villages in the area. Some of these Christian villages trace their lineage all the way back to the time of Christ. To no longer be able live on their land was unthinkable. Still, they had no way to drive out a large group of heavily-armed soldiers. So they moved on. There was another Christian village nearby called Gish. Thus began the long, cold walk.

As they walked into Gish, their skin began to crawl. Something wasn't right. Even the hillsides were barren as they approached the village. Normally, the shepherds would have welcomed them. There were no shepherds. As they entered the village, the expected buzz of people was not there. There were no people. As they walked farther into the village, they found a few elderly people. They were all that was left of the village. The Zionist soldiers had been here, too.

Their story was different. These soldiers didn't even bother to manufacture a story about protecting the village from danger. They simply removed the people at the point of a gun — actually, many guns. The few elderly members of the village they encountered had not been worth the soldiers' time to drive off. There was a strange detail to this story that was different from their own. One of the old men in Gish was convinced that the Zionist soldiers were in a hurry because, when the last group of villagers was run off, he heard gunfire. He believed that this had expedited their evacuation. He thought they'd fled to Lebanon.

Unfortunately, it would be the boy that would unlock the mystery of where those people went. Time was an unnerving force. When would the soldiers that had forced them out of their village of Biram find them in Gish? The boys found a deflated soccer ball, and for a moment in time they were happy. Well, they were distracted. In their excitement, someone kicked the ball out of bounds. The boy ran after it. It was a normal instinct. He was the young one. The ball came past him, so he ran after it. The result was anything but normal. The sand that the ball had come to rest upon was loose. It looked as if it had been disturbed recently. But he was just a boy. After all, there was a ball to return. But there was that odor. But he needed to get the ball. And then there was that twig protruding from the sand near the ball. It was an odd color. He should just get the ball. But he was a curious boy. He pulled at the twig. There was that odor again. The twig didn't come loose immediately. So he grasped the twig and pulled hard. As the remainder of the twig surfaced it became clear it wasn't a twig. The swollen blue portion of the finger rose from loose sand. It was attached to a small hand and arm. A boy's hand and arm. A young boy like him. A Christian Palestinian boy like him. A boy from a small powerless village like his. He couldn't even scream.

When others arrived, they gave a proper burial to the boy and the 23 bodies that lay next to him, that the loose sand barely covered. Apparently the gunfire that the old man had heard was not simply a warning to these villagers. The boy could not return to the sandlot.

These former residents of Biram sheltered themselves from the winter elements in the homes of the former residents of Gish. The parallels were not lost on them. As more and more villages suffered the same fate as theirs, they heard news from refugees. Zionist militants had taken a munitions factory and were attacking the British as well as the Palestinians. They were now well-equipped with heavy weapons. Some small groups of Palestinian villagers had tried to resist, but they were overwhelmingly outgunned.

They also heard stories about the United Nations taking up the *Palestine question*. They didn't know Palestine was a question. They had been living in Palestine for as many generations as anyone can remember. They had hoped that the more powerful nations of the world would see their plight and do something to help. Instead, the more powerful nations spoke of partition (dividing the land). The Zionist Jewish immigrants who legally owned 6% of the land would be given 55%. The Palestinians who legally owned 90% of the land would be given 45%. This brought back memories for the boy's father. He remembered talk back in the 1920s from new Jewish immigrants of taking all of Palestine. Following that talk, there had been trouble between the Jewish immigrants and the Palestinians. Now, it seemed as if that talk was becoming reality.

More terrifying news came as winter of 1947 turned into the spring of 1948. Palestinian villages were being bombed. The war had not been declared yet, but things were turning dark. It would've been cold comfort, but perhaps comfort nonetheless, to this boy of eight, to believe that these were just isolated acts of violence by the Zionists. However, statements by Zionist Jewish leaders that called for the land to be purified of the Palestinian people suggested that these attacks were the systematic execution of an overall plan. David Ben-Gurion, said, "after the formation of a large army in the wake of the establishment of the state, we will abolish partition and expand to the whole of Palestine" (Flapan 22). David Ben-Gurion would soon become prime minister of the new state of Israel. He had made the statement 11 years earlier and, in the meantime, he had indeed developed a large army. Other statements by Ben-Gurion at the time suggested he intended to use it. "We must expel Arabs and take their places...and, if we have to use force – not to dispossess the Arabs of the Negev and Transjordan, but to guarantee our own right to settle in those places – then we have force at our disposal" (Masalha 66).

With the spring flowers came news of the massacre in a small village, disturbingly like his own, in many ways. It was called Dier Yassin. Hundreds of Palestinian villagers were killed. The stories that reached the boy's ears were nightmares come to life. The ones involving the mutilation of children were perhaps the most disturbing to the ears of a young boy. He didn't understand why the Zionist Jewish immigrants from Europe were different than his Jewish neighbors. His Jewish neighbors were outraged and saddened by these events.

In May of 1948, the British gave up control of Palestine. As they left, David Ben-Gurion declared the establishment of the new state of Israel, thus claiming the 55% of Palestine from the never-agreed-to partition plan and positioning the new Israeli military to take much more. The conflict moved from a civil war to a full-scale one as surrounding Arab states joined the conflict. Though they were fighting the newly-declared Israel, many of the Arab states did not have the Palestinians' interest as a top priority.

The boy was not aware of all of this. He simply knew that he was entering his second winter as a refugee in the village of Gish. He knew that they couldn't return to their village because the Zionist Jewish soldiers, now called Israelis, would get them. But how long until the Israeli soldiers showed up at this village? Many Palestinians faced the same paralyzing fear. During the conflict, three-quarters of a million Palestinians will flee to other countries where many remain as refugees to this day.

The boy did not have to wait long for his answer. With the sweet smells of spring came the ominous rumble of military trucks. The metallic edge of the voice on the loudspeaker sliced through the calm of the morning. The voice demanded that all the men and older boys come out of their homes. The soldiers leveled their guns as the men slowly came out of their homes with their sons. Tears and terror choked the boy as he saw his father and three of his brothers walk toward the soldiers. His father calmly told his sons that it would be all right, but the boy knew it wasn't all right. This is how it must have started with the previous villagers of Gish. He could still remember the boy's hand protruding from the loose sand. That boy had walked the same path.

The soldiers began to yell at the men demanding they give up their guns. The men stood like this hour after hour. They were allowed no water under the Middle Eastern sun. They were not allowed to use the bathroom. The morning passed into afternoon, and still they stood. There were no guns to give up. Men fainted from heat exhaustion, and still it went on. The boy watched his sweat-drenched father barely standing but subtly moving his lips in silent prayer. The boy knew that his father wasn't praying for himself or even his family. He was praying for the soldiers. The boy had heard his father pray night after night as he gathered the family for prayer: "Forgive them, oh God. Heal their pain. Remove their bitterness. Let us show them your peace."

As the sun began to set, the men were told to return to their homes. Seeming to know what was next, his father fought off the exhaustion and sat with each one of his children one last time. Again, the loudspeaker shattered the silence. All the men were to be loaded onto trucks. "We are taking your terrorists away. This is what happens to all terrorists. You will not see them again," the metallic voice rang out.

Fifty-nine years later, the boy asked me in an interview, "How can we be the terrorists? We are the terrified. We are not born with stones or bullets in our hands. That is taught" (Chacour).

The tragedies of this boy's life could fill several books. That is not the focus of this book. It's about the choices made in spite of these tragic events: *these bones*. Here lie the bones, the brick-and-mortar, on which to build another tragic figure – one who would feel justified in taking another's life whether man, woman, or child. Whether it's an Israeli pilot firing a missile into a crowded village or a Palestinian suicide bomber detonating in a crowded mall, it's the same tragic result: more bones, more building blocks.

This has become the dominant narrative we hear in America night after night. But what if the boy walked away from the bones? What if he refused to pick them up, to lay the foundation of his own unique tragedy? Interestingly, this story is the story of many, if not most, Palestinians, but most don't pick up the bones and build a tragedy. A small number do. Some understandably choose to walk away from the bones and start a new life in another country. Many quietly resist the brutality of the bones by remaining where they are and living a life of quiet dignity among the bones. A few transcend the bones. This few, remarkably, is larger than those who choose the path of violence. The tragedy here in the United States is that we seldom, if ever, hear about the few. This few heroically transcend the bones by nonviolently engaging those who are supposed to be their enemies, and in transcending the bones, the bones are shattered. This boy was one of the few.

This boy born of tragedy will ultimately lead to many international peace awards and the nomination for the Nobel Peace Prize three times. In 1994, he received the prestigious World Methodist Peace Award. In 2001, he was the recipient of the Niwano Peace Prize (Mar Elias). The path of peace was long, difficult, and scattered with many bones. This path led through an orphanage in Haifa to schooling in Nazareth. He studied theology in Paris and returned to his troubled homeland in 1965 to be ordained a priest. He didn't run away from the fire. He walked back into it. He was assigned to a village that was troubled, too, divided by old wounds and hatreds that bubbled up continually from its history. Within a few years, he united the village, and the people began calling him Abuna, a term of endearment meaning, father. He then opened a school for young children, a day care center, and several community centers that served the desperate needs of the entire region. Without facilities for the school, day care center, or staff, he used his own home. This resulted in him spending most nights sleeping in the back of his VW Beetle.

As the 1967 War came, the Israelis were able to extend their military control from the 75% they controlled after the 1948 war, to 100% of Palestine. They extended military control over the Palestinians in the West Bank and Gaza. The wound between Palestinians and Israelis was yet again deepened. It was a short war, but much carnage can be achieved in a small amount of time. The Israeli military struck without warning, destroying 400 planes on the ground, defeating the surrounding Arab countries in only a few days. But, as usual, the Palestinians paid the highest price. Four hundred thousand new Palestinian refugees were created. The Palestinians in the West Bank and Gaza were now brought under the control of the Israeli military, making their situation far worse than Palestinians like Father Chacour, who were absorbed into Israel after the 1948 war.

❧ THE MARCH ❧

After the 1967 War, Father Chacour started looking for ways to give the people hope. Not simply *his* people but all the people: both Palestinian and Israeli. The goal was to give both groups hope that there could someday be reconciliation between them. One of the demonstrations he led illustrates this quite powerfully. It took 18 months and quite a bit of courage and faith on both sides to organize. He received many supportive letters from his Jewish Israeli friends, but it wasn't clear that when it came time, they would march with him. One letter read, "among the rabbis, many I know are afraid that Golda Meier (Prime Minister of Israel at that time), like Jezebel, has sold herself 'to do evil' to your people." Afterwards, the rabbi quickly stated that he couldn't have his name associated with some of the statements in this letter.

Chacour symbolically designed the demonstration route to be the same path as the victory parade from the 1967 War that had wounded these people so deeply. He remembered the victory parade. He remembered watching through tears of disbelief as Christian priests, nuns, and ministers celebrated the war machines as they rolled by. They applauded the war as a fulfillment of prophecy. He shared his fellow clergy's love for his Jewish brethren, but to celebrate the tragedy of the victims was inconceivable.

More buses were arriving. Thousands of Palestinians had committed to the march and now were arriving in bus after bus. What about all his Jewish friends who wrote in support? Would they show up? Would this be a joint demonstration? It was nearing the time when the march was scheduled to begin. A few cars arrived, and some of his friends from Hebrew University emerged. It was nice to see them, but it wasn't enough. Minutes later, dozens were arriving on foot. Hope rose in his chest. Around the corner came groups of Muslims and Druze. It was coming together. Priests and rabbis praying together. Jewish men handing out signs saying, "Justice for Biram" and "Justice for the Palestinians." It was hard to believe. He rode in the jeep, megaphone in hand, giving orders to the huge crowd behind him. Christians, Muslims, Jews, and Druze marched as one to ask for peace. They were 8,000 strong as they marched up to the stone steps of the Knesset. They asked for a meeting to talk about reconciliation between Palestinians and Israelis with Prime Minister Golda Meier. If she chose not to meet with them, those that were able would fast, pray, and wait. She chose not to meet with them. It was August in the Middle East, and the heat was brutal. The prayer vigil went on. The response from Golda Meier was a deafening silence. The Jerusalem police chief said it was the most amazing demonstration of unity that he'd ever seen. After four days, the silence from the Prime Minister was complete. Father Chacour called an end to the vigil and fast.

The feeling of failure settled deep into his chest as he walked away from the steps of the Knesset. Just then a Jewish friend from the Hebrew University stopped him and said, "Look there." He pointed to the group of young men standing on the steps of the Knesset with their arms around each other. They were Jewish, Muslim, Christian, and Druze. "Change is here. It's happening in the people's hearts," his friend said.

⚝ THE SCHOOL ⚝

Years later, he stood in front of an Israeli judge. "Your honor, this priest has flagrantly violated the law in building without a permit. We ask your honor to order this illegal building destroyed," the prosecutor stated (Chacour; Chacour and Jensen).

Father Chacour stood alone across from the prosecution's team. The judge directed his gaze to Father Chacour: "You are building without a permit. This is a very serious matter. What have you to say to the court?"

Father Chacour turned toward the judge, straightened himself, and said, "Your honor, our children's education is indeed a very serious matter, yet the authorities refused to grant a permit to build a school. Your Honor, I request time to find a good lawyer. An international crisis about this problem could create many difficulties. We do not need more stains on Israel's reputation. Therefore, I need time to find an excellent lawyer to help us all."

"How much time? Three months? Four months?" the judge asked. Father Chacour was rather shocked. It was rare for a Palestinian to receive this generous of treatment in an Israeli court. "Five months?" the judge again questioned. "Father Chacour, I give you five months to find a lawyer and return to court. Then I want to close this file once and for all." At this, the judge stood and left.

Father Chacour was overwhelmed. In five months' time, the school could be finished, and children would be laughing and studying together in its classrooms. The school was not legal yet, but at least it wouldn't be demolished for the next five months. After that, all bets were off (Chacour; Chacour and Jensen).

I wish I could say this type of situation doesn't happen anymore. But it does. Father Chacour stood in that courtroom in 1982. As I write these words 26 years later, I can tell you from personal experience that it still happens in alarming numbers. Since 1967, in the West Bank and Gaza alone, 18,000 homes have been destroyed by the Israeli government, according to the Israeli Committee Against Housing Demolitions (The Israeli Committee Against House Demolitions ICHAD Website). This figure only includes the 25% of Palestine that the Israelis have controlled since 1967. This does not include the other 75% of the land controlled since 1948. Nor does it include the estimated 400 to 500 entire villages that were destroyed or de-populated in the 1948 War (Khalidi).

Khalidi's book contains a rather encyclopedic account of these tragic events, but it was a remarkably frank quote from a famous Israeli leader of the time, that caught my attention.

"Jewish villages were built in the place of Arab villages. You do not even know the names of these Arab villages, and I don't blame you because geography books no longer exist, not only do the books not exist, the Arab villages are not there either. Nahlal arose in the place of Mahlul; Kibbutz Gvat in the place of Jibta; Kibbutz Sarid in the place of Huneifis; and Kefar Yehushu'a in the place of Tal al-Shuman. There is not one single place built in this country that did not have a former Arab population."

Father Chacour's struggle for a building permit had started a year earlier. He had spent years observing the desperate need for schools among Palestinian youth. His home of Galilee had been under the direct control of the Israelis for over three decades now, but the needs of the Palestinian Israeli children had not been given the same attention as that of Jewish Israeli children, even though the Palestinians here were now citizens of Israel, unlike their more recently conquered brothers in the West Bank and Gaza. He'd already built schools for younger children and community centers, so why not a secondary school so they can finish their education?

I still remember discussing this with him in my 2007 interview. He said to them at the time, "If you let me build a school now, I can save you from having to build a prison later." I reflected on my own childhood and thought about how a bunch of bored, angry young men hanging out with nothing to do, was never a good idea. Most of the amusing stories from my past that resulted in police involvement, started with someone saying "Hey, I'm bored. How about we do _____?" Now take that natural predilection in young males and move it from the stable America of my youth in the 1980s, to a place where these young people witness violence and humiliation regularly. His point was well taken. His vision for the school fascinated me. One would expect him to be focused on the very serious problems of the Palestinian youth that surrounded him, and that would be an admirable goal. Yet he was interested in educating children from all different groups: Christian, Jewish, Muslim, Druze. Beyond this, he wanted to provide them with teachers from all of these groups. He wanted to "have children from all groups write the history of their future together," he told me in an interview (Chacour).

It's hard to imagine anyone saying, "No," to the dream of a school where all different types of children in a conflict zone are encouraged and taught to build their future together without violence. Yet, many powerful people did say no and, indeed, much more. The Israeli government denied him a permit to build the school and told him that he would never get a permit. This, in spite of the fact that he had privately raised the funds necessary. An official privately told him that it would be impossible to build into the rocky slope he had chosen, but he did. He was told it would take five years. He told them he would do it in two. After trying in vain to legally obtain a permit, he broke ground. His crew was entirely made up of volunteers. As they worked, the police arrived.

The police officer approached and demanded, "Who is responsible here?" To this demand, Father Chacour stepped forward and presented himself.

"Where's your building permit?" the officer asked.

"I don't have one," Father Chacour responded.

"How can you build without a building permit?"

"Sir, I don't build with permits. I build with sand, cement, cinder blocks, steel, and wood, not with permits."

"But you cannot do that. You cannot build without a permit in a democratic, civilized country."

"If this country were civilized and democratic, you would've given me a permit for a school long ago. I applied, and you refused. We need a lot more schools in Israel so you can learn to give permits in the future."

"This is not my problem. You have to stop the work. All your men must come with us to the police station."

"No, I will come with you, because I am the only one responsible. These are all volunteers, working without pay" (Chacour; Chacour and Jensen).

Ultimately, the 30 villagers who volunteered that day were arrested. This will happen again and again in his life. Father Chacour will press on through police harassment, serious personal injuries, sabotage, death threats, and much more. In the long run, the school will be completed. He will go on to build or be involved in the creation of an amazing list of institutions.

The following is a partial list:

- Myriam Bawardi Youth and Adult Center in Ibillin
- Myriam Bawardi Kindergarten
- Community and Youth Center in Maylia
- Saint John Chrysostomus Secondary School and Youth Center in Jish
- Saint Joseph Community Center and Youth Center in Tarshiha
- Boy Scouts Center in Shefa'amr
- Community Center in Fassuta
- Community Center in Isifya
- Eight public libraries, containing over 150,000 volumes
- A Summer Camp for children that has grown from 1,129 children to reach more than 5,000 young people of different religions and denominations from 30 different villages in the Galilee region
- Prophet Elias High School in Ibillin
- Prophet Elias Technological College
- Center for Religious Pluralism at Mar Elias College
- Mar Elias Teachers' Regional Resource Centre
- Myriam Bawardi Elementary School
- Mar Elias University (Mar Elias)

Mar Elias Educational Institutions, as his complex has come to be called, now serves approximately 4,000 students. That's not bad for a guy who started his first institution sleeping in the back seat of his VW Beetle. There are so many more stories about this remarkable man that I could tell, but they are told in much greater detail in previous works about him, such as "Blood Brothers." In a sense, he is the most well-known of the people I will write about in this book. Most of the people in this book have no books written about them, unlike Father Chacour. Most are lucky if they can get newspaper coverage, which is curious given their incredible stories. Indeed, I was very hesitant to even include Father Chacour in this book for, although his story is remarkable, it's already been told. However, I felt it was necessary to lay out, for the uninitiated reader, some of the important events in the Palestinian Israeli conflict that led us to today's situation.

Father Chacour's life provides a great opportunity to do just that. His life begins in an environment that we find hard to imagine: Palestinians and Jews living in peaceful coexistence. Clearly, this wasn't the case everywhere. When European Jews started immigrating to Palestine in the early 20th century, there were disputes over land in many areas. However, even in those areas, it was decades before any large-scale violence took place. This conflicts with our notion of the Middle East as an inherently violent place. This is why Father Chacour, as an eight-year-old boy, was shocked by his new experience with these Zionist Jewish soldiers. His frame of reference had been the Jews in neighboring villages that had been their friends. Indeed, previous to the immigration of European Jews to Palestine in the late 19th century, early 20th-century, non-European Jews had always existed in Palestine in small numbers. Their record of violence with Palestinians was very rare, especially when you compare it to that of Europe during the same time period.

I often ask my students why this conflict started. A typical response is, "Muslims hate Jews, and Jews hate Muslims." We then go back to the beginning of the conflict in the late 19th century, and I ask them to "remind me again where the European Jews were running from?" "Europe," comes the response. "Okay. What is the dominant religion of Europe?" "Christianity" comes the unblinking response, not yet seeing the irony. "Okay. So they ran from Christian Europe to where?" I ask. "The Ottoman Empire," comes their response. I then ask, "and its dominant religion was?" They reply, "Islam of course." At this point, you can almost hear an audible click as it dawns on a few of them. For the rest, I ask the question hanging there in the air. "So right before this conflict started, the European Jews were running from the persecution in Christian Europe into the arms of a Muslim empire? How does this make sense if Jews always hated Muslims and Muslims always hated Jews?"

The short answer is, it doesn't. This conflict has always been about land. Yes, over the years of this horrible conflict, Muslims have learned to hate Jews and vice versa, but the same can be said for Palestinian Christians and Jews. Religion has been used recently to inflame the conflict and rally people politically, but the center of the issue remains the land. Here again Father Chacour's childhood mirrors this. He is eight years old when the United Nations offers the Palestinians 45% of the country they owned 90% of, while giving 55% to the Jewish immigrants who owned 6% of the land.

This Palestinian boy could not understand what happened. Most of the adults couldn't either. They couldn't understand why their land was being taken from them to pay for the horrendous sins committed in Europe against the Jewish people. You can see Chacour's father's sympathy and willingness to help the Jewish immigrants. He died never understanding why he could not go back to his land. He even worked his own land as a day laborer simply to be on his land, even though he could no longer own it. One can see the beauty of this man's openness in his son's legacy. I've heard Father Chacour say several times to the Israelis, "You are welcome to live with us *but not without us.*" He simply requests to be afforded the same rights as other Israeli citizens. This is a remarkably benevolent statement for someone who as a boy watched the Israeli military destroy his village on Christmas Day. This was the day they promised to give it back.

Father Chacour lives through the 1948 war that resulted from the inequitable UN Partition Plan, and suddenly the Zionist Jewish immigrants are transformed into the Israelis. When the smoke clears, they control 75% of the land, including his home. He grows to be a man and watches another war in 1967 where the Israelis gain control over the last 25% of Palestine in the West Bank and Gaza. Here the legacy is even more difficult. Most of these Palestinians will not become citizens and will live under military occupation for decades. Today, the West Bank still does.

Father Chacour's life illustrates another theme of this book. The myth that the Palestinians and Israelis all hate and fear each other, is challenged again in Chacour's story. Father Chacour clearly meets Israeli soldiers who exhibit the hatred and fear Palestinians have come to expect, but he also meets an Israeli judge who goes out of his way to help him move forward with his school and Israeli friends who march with him for peace and justice. Through my research on this book, I've met Israeli after Israeli who were sympathetic to the plight of the Palestinians. Many of them try to improve the situation at great personal cost to themselves. Conversely, I am truly taken aback by how many Palestinians, many of whom have suffered tremendous tragedies, do not hold this against the Israeli people. They criticize the Israeli government policy, not the Israeli people.

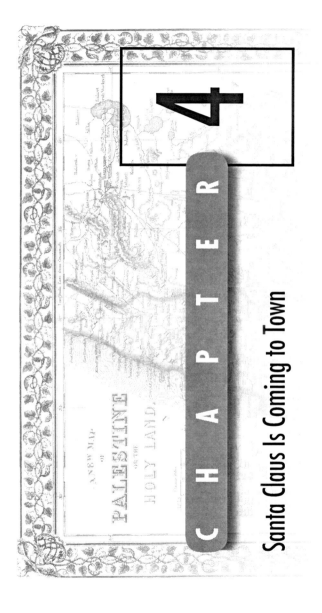

CHAPTER 4

Santa Claus Is Coming to Town

Santa's coming to town. The imagery here is so iconic, that as you read these words you'll probably have some memory, image, or song in your head. I personally have Michael Jackson's pre-pubescent voice squalling through my head from the Motown version of the song "Santa Claus is Coming to Town." This is really my wife's fault. Her brother is more of a Motown fan than I am. But I digress. As I said: Santa is coming to town.

Of all the towns in the world, it's Bethlehem, and of all the times of the year it could be, it's Christmas. It's a postcard waiting to happen. Now I'm a historian, and yes, I realize that the legend of Santa doesn't really connect very well with Bethlehem. But you have to admit that, if you're willing to overlook some of the historical facts regarding this story, we really have the Christmas trifecta here. He's even got a bag of candy. Here's where the picture falls out of focus. Santa arrives, candy bag in hand, to be beaten and then arrested by a large group of soldiers with machine guns in hand. The scene is truly surreal. I don't mean surreal in the fashionable way that many people use it today, as essentially a synonym for the word, weird. I mean surreal in the way you learned back in college, where fur grows out of the side of a coffee cup.

Why has Santa come all the way from the North Pole for a beating? Well, he came to see a man about a wall. As troubled as the past has been between the Palestinians and Israelis, today's realities have their own unique brutalities for the Palestinians of the West Bank. 1948 brought a catastrophe that took much of their land. 1967 brought Israeli soldiers to occupy the West Bank and control their movement. Now, the little bit of land they have left to live on, is being systematically taken from them by Israeli walls and settlements. A Palestinian man I know in East Jerusalem, described his lack of faith in the peace process this way: "The Oslo peace process brought us the settlements. The Roadmap brought us the Wall. Perhaps the next peace process will put a roof on those walls and finish us off for good."

It is amazing to watch the changes over my different trips to the West Bank. During my first trip, the Israeli soldiers on the streets and the snipers on rooftops were indeed intimidating. But in my 2006 trip, I received my first up-close-and-personal look at the Wall as I entered Bethlehem. The picture I took of it is on the cover of this book. The banner in the picture makes a fascinating statement: "Peace be with you" from the Israeli Ministry of Tourism is written on the 24-foot wall next to a 30-foot gun/observation tower. What does this imply? "Peace be with you." Don't worry; we've got all the bad guys locked up? Why is it in Arabic? Just to rub it in? As a warning to Israeli Arabs? Or does the government really mean it? Is this the only vision of a secure future? Who's *they*? It's important to distinguish. Many Israelis are fighting hard against this policy. They will be discussed later in the book. They would be upset if I said that this Israeli government policy reflected their views. It does not. There are many Jews worldwide who are not Israeli and find this policy repugnant. There are also many Israelis inside the country who don't really know much about it. I took a group of Americans to Israel in 2008. As we traveled from Bethlehem, where the Wall is very clear, to Jerusalem's Mount of Olives, they were struck by the fact that it was very difficult to see the Wall at all in the tourist areas of Jerusalem. In the places in Israel where you can see the Wall, a program has begun to coat the Israeli side of the wall with beautiful Jerusalem stone so that it doesn't look as bleak as the Palestinian side of the wall. So why did Santa Claus come at this particular time? This beautiful wall is being built on Palestinian land and is separating the village from 60% of its farm fields.

Santa came to march in the frontline of a peaceful procession of these people back onto their own land, if only for a moment. They do this every Friday like thousands of other Palestinians across the West Bank. They ask for something that is completely unacceptable to the Israeli military: to stand on their own land for a moment.

As Santa and the people who followed him approached the land, it was clear that things would get ugly. An Israeli soldier immediately grabbed Santa by the throat. Santa had no opportunity to protect his throat because, like all the people in the march, he walked arm-in-arm with people on his left and people on his right. One reason the demonstrators did this was to show the soldiers that it was a peaceful demonstration. The soldier that grabbed Santa clearly didn't realize the symbolic value of having a photo taken where you have Santa locked in a death grip. His commander did. After he noticed the press cameras, he signaled to the soldier, and the soldier threw Santa back into the line of demonstrators (Awad).

At this point, the two sides adopted a familiar position. The demonstrators locked arm-in-arm with Santa in a line. Nose-to-nose with this line are the soldiers. A strange line dance begins as the demonstrators try to walk toward the land and the soldiers shove them backwards. This dance often degenerates from shoves into beatings. The demonstrators are trained not to respond with force or even verbally say anything insulting to the soldiers, as they are being beaten.

Ironically, Santa has told me that, in general, the only time the rule about verbal abuse is broken, is when they have Israeli peace activists that join the Palestinian demonstrations. Speaking as someone who's been in a few intense confrontations like this, this is not a criticism of these Israeli activists on my part. I have lost my temper before and have no right to criticize. I simply find it ironic. You have to keep your sense of humor in this environment, or the tragedy of it all will quickly and inevitably overwhelm you.

There are different schools of thought on nonviolence. This group that meets every week near Bethlehem believes strongly in not only no physical violence, but no verbal abuse either. The ultimate goal of this protest is not simply to stand on your own land once a week, but to change hearts and minds by *how* they do what they do.

Santa saw a group of soldiers looking toward a different part of the demonstrators' line. He had learned to observe facial expressions and nonverbal behavior, to predict what the soldiers would do next in these situations. In a previous demonstration, he had predicted that the soldiers were about to fire on the crowd before they did. Remember, "He knows when you've been sleeping. He knows when you're awake. He knows when you've been bad or good. So be good for goodness sake."

The soldiers had focused their gaze on one particular Palestinian in the group. In previous demonstrations, he'd been a leader, directing the group with a bullhorn. As a result, the soldiers targeted him. This is not uncommon in these demonstrations. I've heard similar stories over and over again. People perceived to be leaders of these peaceful demonstrations are not only singled out for rougher-than-average beatings, but also are reportedly shot by snipers' rifles with *rubber bullets* in the head. This violates Israeli military regulations, but it has been observed many times (Friends of Freedom and Justice Bilin Official Website; The International Solidarity Movement Official Website).

The group of soldiers surged toward the man they perceived to be a leader in the demonstration. Santa leapt in between the soldiers who had grabbed hold of the man to prevent him from being harmed. He's actually pretty spry for a mythical figure who has the reputation for shopping at the big-and-tall stores. If you'd like to see this surreal moment captured on film for all time, I recommend you go to this website: Reuters.com or Holy Land Trust.com.

While Santa was successful in preventing the man from further injury, he was not so fortunate himself. The soldiers turned their wrath on Santa. At the end of the encounter, Santa had many bruises to show for his decision to intervene. With the demonstration devolving into a beating, Santa had the demonstrators retreat to a sustainable position while he handed out candy. Remember, the key here is hearts and minds. It's not only about trying to protect your people from serious injury; it's about keeping the protest nonviolent and trying to protect the soldiers from themselves. This last point sounds silly. Why would soldiers need protection from themselves, and how is an unarmed man going to do it? To answer that question, I need to explain a bit about the man in the Santa suit and the nature of nonviolence.

The man in a Santa suit is Sami Awad. He's the leader of an organization known as The Holy Land Trust. In addition to leading nonviolent demonstrations, he and his organization conduct nonviolent training sessions throughout the West Bank. One of their more remarkable success stories involves members of the Al-Aqsa Martyrs Brigade, one of the more violent Palestinian resistance groups fighting the Israeli occupation.

The group of 25 of them approached Sami about training. Rather than accepting them without question, he challenged them. Sami questioned whether or not they had the courage necessary for nonviolent protest. Keep in mind, these men use weapons for living, and Sami doesn't even have a Santa suit to protect him. Sami pressed on. "It takes more courage," Sami said. "You fired machine guns at the Israeli tanks as they invaded Bethlehem in 2002, but then you had to retreat, because you were outgunned. Nonviolence requires you to stand right there in front of the tank and not retreat. Do you have this kind of courage?" (Awad)

Here's the amazing thing, they didn't shoot him for suggesting they might not have the guts for his kind of work. In fact, 25 of them signed up for the training and have not engaged in violence since. Let me say that again for those of you in the cheap seats — they "have not engaged in violence again." If you spent a lot of time in this region or even studied it a bit, this should amaze you.

He currently has 45 trainers in the West Bank. In 2007, he received a request to train members of Hamas in nonviolence. He successfully trained 20 of their West Bank leaders and was set to do the same in Gaza, when political conditions on the ground spun out of control. As a result, those plans are now on hold.

This is Sami; on the one hand training leaders of Hamas in nonviolence, while on the other hand, he's trying to protect and see the humanity in these Israeli soldiers who just assaulted him twice. In the different interviews I conducted with Sami, I've never had the chance to ask him, but I think he'd agree with Father Chacour's statement about policemen (in this case about soldiers):

> Israeli police have something in common with American, Russian, Palestinian, and even Nazi police. Everywhere, unmistakably, behind the uniform is a human being. The problem is how to strip the uniform from the officer to discover the humanity and the beauty. Sometimes the humanity is nearly suffocated by the uniform, as in Nazi Germany. Nevertheless, we teach our children that even when the Jewish Israeli soldiers are humiliating, torturing, and killing Palestinians, as in the West Bank and the Gaza Strip, there are human beings behind the ugly faces and uniforms of the soldiers. The problem is how to strip away the atrocities and the violence, converting the soldiers to the beautiful persons they can be (Chacour and Jensen).

Sami tries to lead demonstrations in such a way that he can tap into that human side. Allowing soldiers to see the Palestinians as humans, as opposed to enemies, can prevent them from going down the path of regularly committing violence against unarmed demonstrators. That path disconnects them from their own humanity. It leads only to pain on both sides. Young Israeli soldiers are frequently put into morally untenable situations where they are expected to do brutal things to Palestinians. This will be discussed in more depth in the next chapter. In mistreating the Palestinians under their control, not only are they treating Palestinians as subhuman, but in the process, they often lose touch with their own humanity.

Sami has described seeing Israeli soldiers breaking down and crying during demonstrations due to the internal conflict over what they were ordered to do. When he said this, I was reminded of the soldier I met at the checkpoint during my first trip to the Middle East, who said, "When I'm done with my service, I will move far away from here and never think again on what was done in this place." As I said, Sami's tactics try to protect the soldiers from themselves.

Think about how many of our expectations or assumptions shatter. Our typical reaction as a human is to protect me and mine. That is understandable, but this philosophy asks you to go beyond that to protect all humans — including your enemy. How does this line up with our assumptions about the Middle East? In America, we view it as an inherently violent place. This view is continually reinforced by the images we are exposed to. Yet here is a peaceful group that is part of a larger movement, numbering in the hundreds, that walks out every week knowing full well that they will likely be beaten, shot, and gassed. In spite of this, one of their main goals is to protect the soldiers from themselves. Why?

Nonviolence aims to send a message to the world about the injustice that the Palestinians face daily. However, that message is not simply aimed at an external audience in Europe or the United States. The message is intended for the soldiers themselves. If the soldiers can indeed be reached and shown that what they're doing to these people is wrong, real change can be accomplished on the ground. This is the kind of change that can end a conflict, even one as brutal as this.

In situations like this, we often view power rather simplistically. The government has the soldiers and the guns, and therefore at the end of the day, no matter what the protesters do, the government wins. Nonviolence views the situation in a more complex way. Soldiers can shoot, beat, and gas the protesters. But what happens if, after all of this, the protesters come back again and again and yet again. The Israeli military has a long history of imposing curfews. On my first trip to the West Bank, people were still talking about the one that had lasted nearly two months. More recently, in 2002, the city of Nablus spent nearly 200 days under a curfew which forced them to spend 80% of their time indoors, making simple tasks like obtaining medical treatment and buying groceries very difficult.

What if the people don't stay inside? Not four or five of them that you can arrest but *all* of them? Of course, talking all of the people into doing this, when the cost is a beating, jail time, or your life is difficult, is another matter. But what if you could? Do you, as the military commander, give the order to shoot? Shoot all of them? Shoot Santa Claus, bag of candy in hand? You can't arrest all of them. It forces a moral choice on the part of the military. That's its intent: to force a moral choice not previously contemplated (Gregg 43). Perhaps a choice just waiting to happen? Look at the two soldiers in the previous chapter. One was clearly struggling with this moral dilemma but at the same time trying to bury it. The other soldier still viewed Palestinians as animals. What if he didn't have that stereotype to hide behind anymore? If you shoot, beat, and gas an animal for coming to the same place every week, it will go away. Why do these people keep coming back?

There are clear examples of nonviolence working, that is Mohandas Gandhi, Martin Luther King, Jr., Badshah Khan, etc. Yet there are failures, too. Anti-war organizations such as the Student Nonviolent Coordinating Committee (SNCC) in the 1960s grew impatient with nonviolence and began emphasizing Black Power and the principle of meeting violence with violence. Thus, organizations like the Black Panthers were born. The historical pattern seems to be that once a nonviolent organization makes the choice to respond to violence with violence, they have already lost the struggle. When a nonviolent movement accepts violence, they have conceded that violence is acceptable. Now, it is only a question of who has the greater physical force at their disposal (Kurlansky). So you have now lost the moral high ground and allowed it to turn into a confrontation, where might does make right.

The reason behind this is clear and more than simply moral. John Lennon said it this way, "… to fight the establishment with their own weapons is no good, because they always win, and they have been winning for thousands of years. They know how to play the game of violence, and it's easier for them when they can recognize you and shoot you" (Lennon). They recognize you because now you are acting precisely how they expect you to act, which is how they would act. The moral stance of nonviolence confuses them. It doesn't fit the normal paradigm. It is unclear how they should deal with you. Do they simply shoot unarmed people? It is in their interest to turn the confrontation into a violent one. There, the choice is clear, and they have the advantage. "It is the tactic of state thuggery to reduce the dialogue to the level of thugs" (Kurlansky). If the weaker party responds with violence, they lose. President Eisenhower, by no means an advocate of nonviolence, was very realistic about the nature of violence: "Remember this: when you resort to force as the arbiter of human difficulty, you don't know where you are going; but generally speaking, if you get deeper and deeper, there is just no limit except what is imposed by the limitations of force itself" (Woolley and Peters).

CHAPTER 5

"I Thought I Would Be Fighting Terrorists"

I was standing on the corner in downtown Tel Aviv near Dizengoff Center. I was waiting for an interview. I was scanning the crowds more intently than usual, because I didn't even know what the man I was supposed to meet looked like. He didn't know what I looked like either. So essentially, I was looking for someone who looked like they were looking for someone. My mind drifted for a moment as I remembered the police reports after this area had been bombed by Hamas a few years ago. I was distracted from this memory by the sight of a man with a subtle military bearing, crossing the intersection. Nonverbal communication is a funny thing. When he looked up and became aware of me watching him, I nodded. He returned the nod, and a minute or two later, we shook hands. Within five minutes after that, we were talking about some of the more personal and painful events of his life. He was a refusenik, an Israeli soldier who agrees to perform military service but refuses to serve in the Occupied Territories. The movement began in January 2002 when many Israeli soldiers witnessed the reality of the occupation personally. The group of 50 combat soldiers and officers publicly declared that they would no longer help to "dominate, expel, starve, and humiliate an entire people." They felt they were given "commands and directives that had nothing to do with the security of our country, and that had the sole purpose of perpetuating our control over the Palestinian people" (Courage to Refuse).

As we walked down the street, he told me about his 23 years of military service, beginning with the war in Lebanon and extending through missions in Gaza, where he witnessed Palestinians being beaten and tortured while handcuffed. He's a lot like many of the soldiers who today refuse service in the Occupied Territories, a soldier with a long list of service to his country, conflicted between loyalty to his country and loyalty to his conscience. Do you follow orders when they require you to harm or kill innocent people? Do you follow them when you believe they make your country less secure? But your country is asking. It's your patriotic duty. Isn't it?

Patriotism means that you love your country. Love is an awfully high standard. If I love my family, it means that I'm willing to sacrifice for them and even die for them. I have sacrificed for them, and I would die for them. This type of love implies that I would do what is best for them in spite of the personal cost. So when they are acting in a way that is right, I encourage them. But what about when they don't? My daughters are currently very young, but what about 10 or 15 years from now? What if one of them, God forbid, became a drug addict? Do I encourage that behavior because I love her? Or do I confront this behavior and show her how it can ultimately destroy her?

I believe the higher standard of love means that I take the harder road – the road that calls her behavior into question and will almost guarantee a strained relationship with my daughter in the short run. It seems to me that these soldiers love their country very deeply – so deeply that they are willing to risk that strained relationship with their country. Here, a strained relationship often means being court-martialed and doing time in jail. They are willing to risk this because this is what love of country demands. If soldiers are being asked to follow orders that are not only immoral and harmful to the civilian Palestinian population, but also immoral and harmful to the state of Israel, it is their patriotic duty to refuse. They refuse precisely because they do love their country.

As this former soldier and I drank coffee at an outdoor café, he described his decision to refuse and the time he spent in jail afterwards. Yet, it was his story about attending a demonstration after he was dismissed from the military, that really struck me. It wasn't a grand story. It took only a few minutes to tell. But it was a story that spoke of transformation.

He joined a peaceful demonstration in the West Bank. It was a protest against Israeli occupation. This man walked alongside these Palestinian demonstrators as they marched down the streets of Birziet, signs and flags in hand. Suddenly, tear gas canisters came whizzing over their heads. People were coughing and choking. Then the crack of guns being fired rang out. People fell to the ground on his right and left, struck by steel bullets with rubber coating. It became difficult to see or breathe. People were being beaten to the ground. Fear gripped him, and his reflexes took over. He reached for his cell phone. He must stop this. He must call the police (Lerner).

The weight of the irony hit him like a hammer. For the purposes of our story, it would have been better if he'd actually made the call. Can you imagine being him and making the call to the police, only to hear the police phone ring a few yards away? Through the tear gas, you hear the police commander from your other ear say, hello. Obviously, I'm taking some creative liberties here with the ending of the story. The point is the same. You are raised to believe your country is a democracy. Democracies are founded on law and order. You believe in this so strongly, that you grew up and spent 23 years in the military defending that democracy based upon law and order. You witness events that conflict with your definition of how democracy should act. You voice your concern through peaceful demonstration. Your voice is crushed by the government you fought 23 years to defend. You can't call the police about the people being beaten in the gas-filled streets around you. The police are the ones doing the beating. He suddenly became very aware of the daily life of the Palestinians in the Occupied Territories. One of the last things he said to me, was that he planned to leave his homeland.

The refuseniks are a growing force in Israeli society. Currently, 629 have publicly signed the Combatants Letter: the pledge to refuse service in the occupied territories. Thousands have expressed their support (Courage to Refuse). Below is a copy of the letter:

✂ COMBATANTS LETTER ✂

- **We, reserve combat officers and soldiers of the Israel Defense Forces,** who were raised upon the principles of Zionism, self-sacrifice, and giving to the people of Israel and to the State of Israel, who have always served in the front lines, and who were the first to carry out any mission in order to protect the State of Israel and strengthen it,

- We, combat officers and soldiers who have served the State of Israel for long weeks every year, in spite of the dear cost to our personal lives, have been on reserve duty in the Occupied Territories, and were issued commands and directives that had nothing to do with the security of our country, and that had the sole purpose of perpetuating our control over the Palestinian people.

- We, whose eyes have seen the bloody toll this Occupation exacts from both sides,
- We, who sensed how the commands issued to us in the Occupied Territories destroy all the values that we were raised upon,
- We, who understand now that the price of Occupation is the loss of IDF's human character and the corruption of the entire Israeli society,
- We, who know that the Territories are not a part of Israel, and that all settlements are bound to be evacuated,
- We hereby declare that we shall not continue to fight this War of the Settlements.
- We shall not continue to fight beyond the 1967 borders in order to dominate, expel, starve, and humiliate an entire people.
- We hereby declare that we shall continue serving the Israel Defense Force in any mission that serves Israel's defense.

The missions of occupation and oppression do not serve this purpose – and we shall take no part in them (Courage to Refuse).

I once asked an active duty soldier what he thought of the Refuseniks. His answer was fascinating. "I have a great deal of respect for their courage, but I could never do that."

"Why?" I asked.

"Because I would lose everything."

"What do you mean by everything?"

"I mean *everything*. My family. My friends. My career after the military. Everything."

"How is your career connected to your military service?"

"It's all about connections. If you have a good military record, it opens all sorts of doors for you later in civilian life. If you refuse, those doors are slammed shut."

"Your family and friends would reject you because of your decision to refuse?"

"Yes. We are raised to believe that military service is the highest service you can render to your country. But I never thought I'd be asked to do things like this."

"Like what?" I asked.

"I thought I would be fighting terrorists. People with guns who... you know... shoot back. Not average people who are just working or going to school. Like that woman a little while ago with the bulldozer. I don't know. It's just not what I thought would be." His voice trailed off. He really did not want to talk much about it after this (Anonymous). I couldn't get him to continue and didn't feel right pushing him any further. As we talked, I remembered another Palestinian woman and a bulldozer. Nuha Sweidan was nine months pregnant when the Israeli bulldozer came to demolish the house next to hers in the refugee camp. When her neighbor's house was destroyed, its wall fell and collapsed the wall of her house. Nuha was crushed underneath the rubble. She bled to death as she held her 18-month-old daughter. Her child that was about to be born was killed in the incident as well. I'm not aware of a single mainstream American news source that covered this (Niva).

I'm not sure how the soldiers in that situation emotionally dealt with their actions, but it clearly leaves scars on some soldiers, such as the one I spoke to earlier. Israeli soldiers are forced again and again to make brutal, moral compromises. Over time, there is a price to be paid. One can't ignore things like this without cost. Beyond these more dramatic events I've mentioned, are the day-to-day moral choices which, while not as exciting, must take their toll as well. An organization made up of veteran Israeli soldiers called, Breaking the Silence, illustrates this rather powerfully.

It collects the testimonies of soldiers who served in the Occupied Territories during the Second Intifada. These soldiers witness and participate in military actions that change them fundamentally. Cases of abuse toward Palestinians, looting, and destruction of property have become the norm, and are justified as military necessities or explained as unique cases. These testimonies illustrate that the abuse of Palestinian civilians is systemic and routine. Breaking the Silence makes the case that:

While this reality which is known to Israeli soldiers and commanders exists in Israel's back yard, Israeli society continues to turn a blind eye, and to deny that which happens in its name. Discharged soldiers who return to civilian life discover the gap between the reality which they encountered in the Territories, and the silence which they encounter at home. In order to become a civilian again, soldiers are forced to ignore their past experiences. Breaking the Silence voices the experiences of those soldiers, in order to force Israeli society to address the reality which it created ... We demand accountability regarding Israel's military actions in the Occupied Territories perpetrated by us and in our name (Breaking the Silence Website).

Breaking the Silence has interviewed hundreds of soldiers who served in the territories and continues interviewing soldiers daily. They publish these interviews on their website, in testimonial booklets, through different media outlets, and also through lectures and tours to Hebron. The testimonies are published with minimal editing and with complete confidentiality in order to protect the soldiers and to encourage them to speak (Breaking the Silence).

I've included a few of the testimonies below to illustrate what this *routine* environment can be like. Each story begins with the rank of the soldier and the time and location of the incident. Then the story is told in their own words. The passages in italics are the questions asked by members of Breaking the Silence.

Rank: Officer
Place of incident: Gaza
Description: 2002

I would visit many times in the situation room and in the rooms the lookouts and see all this footage. The first time I was shocked, I saw a movie from the lookout, it showed some old Palestinian farmer that got near, probably by mistake, to the fence. You just see a tank shell that hits him and blows him up. I watched the Palestinian and looked at the soldier who was looking at it and I thought of the soldiers in the tank. When you are out of it, it seems illogical, but when you are inside …

Did anyone say anything about it, anyone who was watching the movie?
No.

It seemed normal?
Yes. When you are inside, it has to seem normal, otherwise, you can't cope.

The theme of this type of situation being normal or routine, comes through clearly in this story. There are many stories I could include here that are extreme and brutal, but that's true of all conflict zones. My point here is to showcase what is normal and commonplace in this particular conflict. When you look at this story and the ones that follow, think about how perverse it is to have this type of behavior be the routine. This is not a battle that lasts a few hours or weeks. It's not even a conventional war that lasts a few years. The Israelis have occupied the West Bank for over 40 years. What does this fearful vision of *normal* do to the Palestinian victims who live in it day after day? What does it do to the Israeli soldiers who are asked to commit acts like this regularly?

Rank: First Sergeant
Unit: Paratroopers
Place of incident: Hebron
Description: None given

Which neighborhood were you shooting at?

Abu-Sneina. All the guys in their posts say: "Wow, everyone is shooting. No one can tell if I'm shooting as well." Everyone was shooting! There was no one who didn't. Once, a friend calls me on the radio and asks: "Meet me in the junction for a sec." I was in one position, and he was in another. I come down to meet him. "Man, you have to get me a magazine, and pick me up. I'm out of bullets." And he didn't have anything to shoot at. He was just watching some area. Just that.

We shot water tanks; we shot windows. For no reason, you know. Sharpshooting. Just for fun.

Was it all in October?

This was in the beginning; in the very beginning, the first weeks, you know. Just shoot for fun, you know. Everyone is shooting, so no one can tell that I'm shooting, too. Everyone is shooting!

I've edited this story because it was too long to include. To read it in its entirety, go to the "routine" section of the Breaking the Silence website. The full story includes more events, both negative and positive. This edited version gives the overall spirit of the piece without going into the stories of blowing up cars and ambulances, and setting fire to civilian buildings.

Here again this story, like the one before it and the one that follows, is from the section of the Breaking the Silence website labeled "routine." The next story shows how the company commander deals with this *normal* behavior.

Rank: First sergeant
Unit: Nachal Charedi
Place of incident: Jordan Valley

There was a company lesson on the subject of going to the border/front and treatment of the Palestinian population. During the lesson, a movie was shown...they showed the movie, and there is a discussion after the movie and the company commander summarizes the discussion. The company commander's grand finale was that "in my previous post as the company commander in the course of the makin, one of the soldiers or the makin there, shot an 11-year-old boy with a rubber bullet, at a distance that is not allowed, from seven meters away or something like that. This boy was killed." And this company commander said that he received (a punishment of) two months or a month in jail, but what the company commander said was don't worry, it will be alright, as you see, even if someone is killed, we know how to take care of you. This is something that demonstrates the importance of a human life. And this was the most inappropriate group to say this to because the Nahal Charedi is the number one magnet of the *hilltop youths* and people with criminal records. We are speaking of IDF fighters that get weapons. They become fighters and they have criminal records on burning cars, shooting into the air during funerals, and all kinds of things. Some of them have been arrested by the general security service in the underground case, that nothing is happening with, and they were released ...

I will let the next few stories speak for themselves.

Rank: Staff Sergeant
Unit: Elite unite of the Nahal brigade

The atmosphere in the unit was "kill, kill, kill; we want to see bodies." This is what they used to say in the briefings, for example in a talk before an operation in Balata [refugee camp], while standing in a tight circle with all our equipment on, the unit commander said that on the one hand there may be losses and we should know how to deal with it, but on the other hand he expected to see bodies. We should come back with dead terrorists. Once he said that his favorite smell is gunpowder discharged from guns. There was another quotation of his about the smell of burning flesh, but I don't exactly remember it.

Rank: First sergeant
Unit: Giv'ati Infantry Unit
Place of incident: Gaza
Description: Middle of 2004

I would go around talking to the guys. I would sit a lot with all of them and talk to them. Surely, we have been to houses we took over for observation missions, we went to all the houses, and in each we talked, sat with the snipers. Sit and talk inside the houses. That's the way they were.

Once we went to *** outpost, on the Philadelphi route. Our aid-company was placed there. I go up – in *** there are cameras on top of the outpost, which record; there is video there. He plays a film for me, and says: "Look. Look what he did today." There is a film there of ... They discovered a tunnel. Ok. They dug the tunnel, bulldozers – they [Palestinians] wanted to dig a tunnel that leads to the outpost. We marked all the 'extermination-zones' to which they [Palestinians] are not allowed to come close. We decided that every one who comes close we shoot a warning shot, and if he doesn't run away, shoot towards the legs. For, after all, this is a residential area.

Whoever comes close to the route?

To the tunnel. Because the tunnel was closer to their area. If they got close to the route they would have been killed. But the tunnel was close to their houses, so it was decided that no one is to come close to the tunnel. Perhaps there is ammunition there; they didn't want them to come close to the tunnel. So one man came close to the tunnel. You could see him. An older person – about 30 or 40 years old.

Unarmed?

No. He wasn't armed. Just walking about – I don't want to say he was innocent, I don't want to make any assumptions. He was walking in the general area of the tunnel. They shot him. He got a bullet here, and fell down.

In the chest.

Yes. He fell down, then stood up, made a few steps, and then dropped dead. I tell them "Why?!" He goes: "No reason, he just got close, they killed him." I say, "Why didn't you shoot his legs? Why the chest? Chest is good, and legs are no good?" – It wasn't from a great distance, and this was a sniper shooting. – "No reason. You know …" I ask, "No one knows about it, right?" – "Obviously not."

How come no one knows?

A sniper is at his post. Also in 'Rainbow in the Clouds' operation, when a sniper shoots, they report shooting.

Does he report what he sees?

He reports shooting. First of all, 'Rainbow in the Clouds' operation was a jungle. There were shootings all the time. One does not have to report shooting. In 'Rainbow in the Clouds' operation there was shooting all the time.

Whose? Both sides?

Yes.

They would shoot at you and you would return fire?

They shot less. We shot more. You know …

Rank: Staff sergeant
Unit: Armored forces
Place of incident: Daharia junction, South Daharia

Palestinians pass through that roadblock on their way to work in Be'er-Sheva. They have to pass; some on foot. Tens of Palestinians a day. One of the officers wanted to keep the order, wanted them to stand in a straight line – like a ruler. He ran beside them and made them straighten up. They didn't do it well enough, so the first person he saw at the beginning – about 50 years old with an 8-year-old kid or something similar, a little boy – the officer shot in the air and they straightened up. And on another occasion …

To straighten up the line?

To straighten up the line. And on another occasion he just beat the hell out of a person … He hit the man's face with the handle of his rifle, kicked him in the groins, spat on him, cursed him – simply went berserk. In front of the man's little boy. He just humiliated him.

Rank: Sergeant
Unit: Nahal brigade
Place of incident: Atarot-Kalandia
Description: 10/2000

There wasn't really a checkpoint in Kalandia [at that time]. We would stand there at the fence of the airport, as if this was aiding the guys who were guarding the airport. There were riots and we would shoot … how do you call it – Rubber [rubber coated metal bullets]. Rubber, stun grenades. And all the time we were playing 'Catch' with the kids throwing stones. We would set traps for them there.

What do you mean by traps?

Traps, let me give you a somewhat funny example. We would put a can with a stun grenade inside, take out the safety pin, and place on it sweets, desserts that we would take from the kitchen. Then the kids would come, look at them and when they picked it up, the grenade would explode in their face. (Citation: This story has been shortened because there were too many interesting stories to include. To read it in its entirety, go to the *routine* section of the Breaking the Silence website. This edited version gives the overall spirit of the piece without going into the stories of rigging couches, etc.)

One way Israeli soldiers deal with this brutal environment is through joining Breaking the Silence and telling their stories. The next chapter deals with another path that some Israeli soldiers choose that takes it a courageous step farther. Some soldiers do more than just refuse.

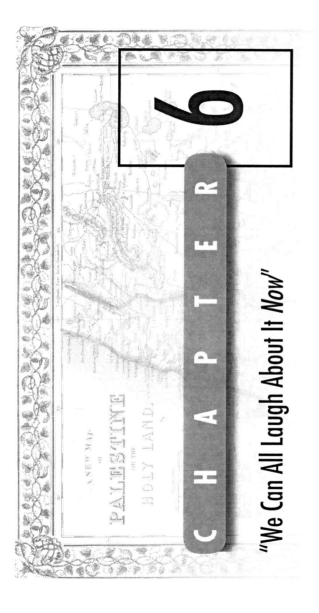

CHAPTER 6

"We Can All Laugh About It *Now*"

It was one of those moments when life brings everything together in one compelling image, that tells the whole story more effectively than words ever could. A former Israeli soldier stood in front of a crowd of Palestinians describing a seminal moment in his life. He and his elite commando unit had invaded a Palestinian village looking for a wanted man. There was screaming and noise. Out of the corner of his eye he saw a panic stricken seven-year-old girl, who had gotten separated from her mother, running toward him. His orders were to stop anyone who was running by all means necessary. She was only a seven-year-old girl, but he had his men to consider. Perhaps she had a bomb. He shouted at her to stop but she kept running. As this young man describes this emotionally-intense scene, the Palestinian man directly to his right translates for the crowd. At this point, a young Palestinian girl from the audience gets up and walks right toward the two men. She was about seven years old from the look of her. With the obliviousness that only a child possesses, she carefully walked right between the two men. To this day I have no idea why she did it. Perhaps she was going to get a drink of water. But as this man described this obviously painful encounter with a seven-year-old Palestinian girl, his hands still in the air from when he described how tall she was, this little girl walked underneath his hands.

You could see the scene in your mind. A terrified little girl, a conflicted soldier, the chaotic sounds of fear in the night. The speaker and the audience were dead silent for a moment. The man had been describing a disturbing incident in a village that all members of that audience knew. Some of them had perhaps grown up there. Most, if not all, had had a terrifying encounter of their own with an Israeli soldier like the one that stood before them now. All of them knew that the Palestinian girl walked beneath his hands. It was a moment that could've turned either way. Fortunately, it turned the right way. Laughter emerged from the crowd as the girl exited the room. The speaker, understandably, was the last in the room to smile, and he did so a bit nervously. Then he said, "Yes, she was about that tall." He paused and gathered himself. Then he said, "We can all laugh about it *now*" (Combatants for Peace).

The man's name was Zohar Shapira. He had been a leader for 15 years in one of the most prestigious commando units in Israeli history. It was the same unit in which legendary figure Ehud Barak had served. He had served on hundreds of missions, many of which took him into the West Bank. He had been told that he was defending his country, but more and more he saw these missions as making Israel less secure, by sowing seeds of hatred again and again. He and 13 soldiers from his unit ultimately wrote a letter to Prime Minister Ariel Sharon refusing to serve on occupation missions that humiliated Palestinians or defended settlements ("For Former Combatants").

The turning point had been the incident he was describing in front of this group of Palestinians. He had fired a warning shot at the girl. She cowered. He had wounded her deeply though the bullet had never touched her. He describes how they looked at one another, not as soldier and enemy, but as two humans. Something inside him snapped.

Zohar went on to become one of the founding members of Combatants for Peace. The group is made up of former combatants, both Israeli and Palestinian, who agreed to put down their arms and fight for peace. In 2005, they began meeting together to tell their stories. Watching these encounters, one is a witness to a fascinating mix of fear, pain, understanding, and acceptance. These men are supposed to hate one another according to their own societies. Yet they find they have far more in common than they could've dreamed.

I first started researching Combatants for Peace in 2006. I flew to the Middle East later that year to conduct some interviews and attend a conference cosponsored by Combatants for Peace in January of 2007. I was staying in a small hotel that I always stay in when I'm in Jerusalem. It's not your typical hotel. It's an old mansion built by an Arab feudal lord many years ago. The restaurant in the basement where I eat breakfast every morning, is a remodeled cellar that's over 300 years old. The second floor of the building where I often stay, was destroyed by Israeli artillery in the 1967 war. I often go to sleep to the sound of traditional music being played on a patio out front, beneath the grape arbor that extends from a single vine. The vine emerges out of the soil in front of the bar. This massive, and no doubt ancient, vine is nearly a foot thick.

I was e-mailing my wife back home from the hotel's one, rather shaky computer, when a child came running into the hotel yelling in Arabic. This, in and of itself, was not that unusual. It is a family-run operation. The family lives in the old house, and everyone who works there is family. However, the child was clearly upset about something. My Arabic skills are not what they should be, but I heard the words Israeli and attack. I stopped to ask the child, "Where did they attack?"

"The place you're going tomorrow," he said and then ran on.

"Ramallah?" I asked.

"Yes," he yelled over his shoulder as he ran into the family quarters.

I ran to find a television. CNN's world edition was showing images of machine gun fire, smoke, and armored personnel carriers overturning cars in downtown Ramallah. I watched

Palestinians scream as they carried their dead and wounded friends out of the streets. This attack was launched as Prime Minister Olmert was conducting peace talks with Egyptian President Mubarak. You get so used to ironies like this that, after awhile, you almost fail to notice them.

I walked out into the café in front of the hotel to see if anyone knew more details than CNN World was reporting. I set up a table near the ancient grapevine. Several people were watching the attack live on laptops. Technology has created some real advantages for those on the weaker side of the conflict. The cameras in cell phones allow us to see human rights abuses, which previously would have gone unrecorded, if someone is willing to stick a camera phone out a window or around the corner, while the war machines roll into town. That being said, no one I knew back in the United States was aware of this invasion until I told them.

I had a difficult decision to make. I had promised my wife that I would try to avoid purposely diving into conflict zones while they were still hot, as I had done in the past. I am a husband and a father now. On the flipside, this meeting in Ramallah was one of the main reasons I'd flown all the way to the Middle East. Without the interviews I could get there, parts of this book would not have been possible. So after a few hours of fitful sleep, I was on the road to Ramallah.

Evidence of the invasion was not hard to find. It was all around me. Yet I had to be somewhat hopeful, considering the meeting I was about to attend. It would be made up of representatives from over 60 peace groups, both Palestinian and Israeli. Many of them would be taking great risks and breaking the law to get here under normal circumstances, let alone coming only hours after an Israeli invasion.

Unfortunately, once I arrived at the meeting, things got off to a less than inspiring start. As impressive as I found that there were over 60 peace activist organizations meeting together to try to solve this conflict, poor planning and bureaucracies have a way of sucking the life out of everything. One after another, each organization was asked to introduce itself to the others. While this looks good on paper, kind of like your standard meeting where everybody goes around and introduces themselves, it doesn't work out that well with so many organizations. If you do a little simple math, multiplying a five-minute introduction times 60 organizations, you can quickly get an idea of how long this well-intentioned, waste of time, took.

As I sat and listened, a man named Jonatan came to the microphone. He represented an organization known as the Freedom Theatre. It's a theater in one of the roughest parts of the West Bank, the Jenin Refugee Camp. It is the only professional venue for theater and arts in the north of the Occupied Territories. It helps Palestinian children heal and express themselves through a unique program of workshops and activities in the theater (The Freedom Theatre).

Jonatan expressed his own frustration with the way the meeting was going from the microphone. Stating that our time would be much better spent planning action rather than sitting around and talking. Here was a man worth talking to. As he walked away from the podium, he took out a pack of cigarettes and headed for the back door where he could smoke. We struck up a conversation just outside the back door of the building underneath an awning, where it was raining heavily. I looked around to see the effects of the Israeli invasion of less than a day before. As we spoke, a bolt of lightning flashed, and the crack of thunder followed quickly on its heels. Jonatan and I both ducked low to the ground. We both rose slowly and looked at each other with a sheepish grin.

"It's not always lightning, you know," Jonatan said.

"I know," I responded with a smile.

Jonatan and I continued our conversation as the rain poured down. We were later joined by a friend of his from the refugee camp. His friend's story was a string of seemingly unending tragedy. It had three of his homes destroyed by the Israeli military. One of his brothers was imprisoned, and the other had been killed, but as he rebuilt his house for the fourth time, he made sure there was room for a computer lab in the basement, so the children of the camp could receive an education. The capacity of some of the people in this conflict to not hate, when it seems so natural, constantly amazes me.

After all of this tragedy, this Palestinian man does not hate Israelis. In fact, his best friend Jonatan is Jewish, and the conference we were at was full of Israelis who he openly embraced. He found their opposition to Israeli government policy inspiring.

As I returned from my talk with Jonatan, I bumped into a group of activists talking to a man from Combatants for Peace. As I listened, I was struck by not only the compelling nature of the story, but also the logical trajectory of any stories such as this. Among all activists there, it seemed to me that they had a unique claim. And after all they had done and seen, if these ex-fighters could come together and talk with one another in a brotherhood of pain, who else could possibly have an excuse not to speak with the other side?

In one of those strange twists of fate, a few days before the incident I described above, a member of Combatants for Peace stood in front of a small group of people and said almost exactly that. His name was Elik Elhanan. In 1995, he had been a highly motivated Israeli soldier. He had never met a Palestinian that wasn't behind the gate at the checkpoint, a day laborer, or a cardboard cutout target at the end of his gun site. In 1997, his little sister was killed in a bombing by a Palestinian militant group on her first day of school (Combatants for Peace).

He felt the feelings of rage and the desire for revenge that one would expect in a tragedy of this magnitude. As these strong emotions rose up inside him, they came into collision with an inconvenient memory one month before he had been slated to go on mission to Lebanon. He was unable to go for administrative reasons. The mission has been declared a success, stating that it killed 11 terrorists. Yet, as he looked at the faces of his friends upon their return, he knew that this wasn't the whole story. As it turned out, they killed three children and two elderly people, not 11 terrorists.

The senselessness of the slaughter of his little sister and the slaughter of innocents on the other side, became intimately connected in his mind. The cycle of endless revenge killings by both sides became clear. "I lost my faith in a military solution," Elik said. "The military doesn't secure us. It gives an excuse to hurt us."

He joined the refuseniks and later became their speaker in France. Ultimately, he felt the movement was limited by its one-sided nature. He wanted to meet the other side. Combatants for Peace gave him the opportunity to do that. He ended his lecture with this statement, which elucidates far more eloquently that thought that went through my mind in Ramallah, a few days later.

"We have to find a different way. And what we are saying is that if we, after all we went through, after all we did, we are able to speak to one another, then anyone can speak and there is no excuse not to do so" (Combatants for Peace).

I don't know a better example of this philosophy lived out in life than Bassam Aramin, a founding member of Combatants for Peace. In January of 2007, his daughter Abir told him in a childlike way, that she would be playing with a friend today after school rather than studying for her exam tomorrow. Bassam, like any father, told her to not even think about it (Aramin).

That afternoon, Bassam's 10-year-old daughter, Abir, left school walking arm-in-arm with her sister and two friends toward home. Israeli border police raced their vehicles into the schoolyard of an adjacent boys school as the girls walked by. The police began firing without provocation according to most witnesses (The Jerusalem Post). The girls began to run away from the soldiers, when Abir's sister saw her fall to the ground as blood splattered on the concrete (Aramin).

Today, Bassam says he would have answered her request to go play with her friends by saying, "Go. Do whatever you want. Play. Because now, she never will. She will never laugh again, never hear her friends calling her name, never feel the love of her family wrapped around her at night like a warm blanket" (Aramin).

Even at a dark moment such as this, when it would be easy to portray things in simple black and white terms, the story defies this dangerous oversimplification. You will see this again and again in this book. Whether one wants to classify all Israelis or all Palestinians as good or bad, or even suggest that they all think in one particular way about each other, everyday reality shatters this myth. The first friend to arrive at the hospital, where Bassam's daughter was fighting for life, was an Israeli. Zohar Shapira, whose story I opened this chapter with, arrived and stayed for three days until Bassam's daughter lost her fight for life.

Those were difficult days for Zohar, too. Bassam's daughter had been like his own. He struggled with his emotions and thoughts of revenge. He wanted to find the soldiers that would shoot children. He admits there's a bit of irony here given his own story. The man that brought him back into focus, surprisingly, was the man who had lost the most. Bassam reminded him that revenge would just open up another circle of vengeance (NPR).

When interviewed, Bassam stated, "It's not a personal problem for Bassam Aramin. 971 Palestinian children have been killed since 2000 with no trial, suspect, or guilty verdict. Abir Aramin is not different. She's like them. But what's different is Abir is my daughter. She belongs to me and belongs to my friends from Combatants for Peace (NPR).

His Israeli friends from Combatants for Peace made it possible to open an investigation into his daughter's death. The Israeli military had tried to blame his daughter for her own death. Bassam says that they first claimed she was among a group of boys throwing stones at the border police (NPR). Most witnesses at the scene claim there were no boys throwing stones (Izenberg). The Israeli military then told Bassam that something blew up in her hands before she could throw it at the police. However, her hands remained in remarkably good shape (NPR). Finally, it was stated that her head injuries must have come from a rock and not a bullet.

Dr. Chen Kugel hired by B'Tselem, an Israeli human rights organization, carried out a forensic examination. The pathologist came to the conclusion that the child had been most likely killed by a rubber-coated metal bullet ("Trigger-Happy"). Bassam believed in justice via the Israeli legal system, not in revenge via the gun. He has not been rewarded for his faith in the system. The Israeli government has closed the investigation for lack of evidence. Yet his reaction to this has been remarkable.

He decided to redouble his efforts for peace in order to protect his other children, as well as those of his Israeli brethren in Combatants for Peace. This what I meant earlier when I called it a brotherhood of pain. He says, "For our children, we choose the difficult path … We don't ask our children to make peace. We want them to enjoy it" (NPR).

I'll end with one last quote that ties together a chapter that began with Zohar, an Israeli, and ends with Bassam, a Palestinian: "I want my daughter to be the last victim. There are partners on the other side who believe what I believe" (Myre). That will be a theme throughout this book. There *are* partners on the other side. In light of what these partners for peace are willing to endure, Elik's statement appears with an even starker relief against the backdrop of apathy we so commonly see surrounding the prospects for peace between the Israelis and Palestinians: " … if we, after all we went through, after all we did, we are able to speak to one another, then anyone can speak, and there is no excuse not to do so."

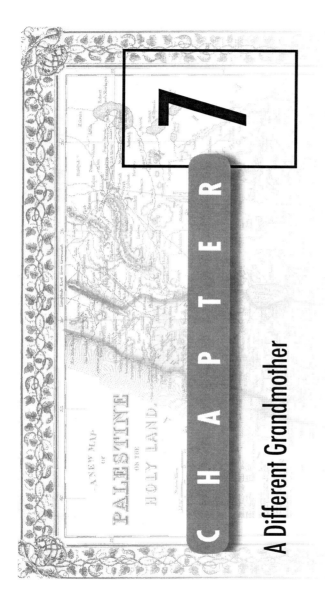

CHAPTER 7

A Different Grandmother

As she discussed the situation with Mahmoud, she shifted effortlessly from Hebrew to Arabic to English. Sometimes this happened within the same sentence. Mahmoud was a Palestinian man across the table from me, whose neighborhood was being threatened by Israeli settlers that broke into their homes. Her name was Neta Golan. She is a legendary Israeli peace activist and a cofounder of the International Solidarity Movement.

As I interviewed her, she dealt with Mahmoud's situation. With one hand, she spoke with an Israeli journalist on the phone. With the other hand, she turned her laptop around to show me the latest headlines from Gaza: "17 people in Gaza killed during an Israeli Military assassination of the son of a Hamas leader." The dead included a 65-year-old woman. I'm sure she was somebody's grandmother. The article went into grisly detail about missing limbs. I stopped reading at that point.

I looked over at Mahmoud as Neta talked to the journalist. His eyes were tired and filled with pain. It's a pain I've seen before, so many times in young and old alike. I thought of a little boy's eyes, a different grandmother, and another assassination.

✂ BALATA REFUGEE CAMP ✂

The little boy screamed uncontrollably as the Israeli soldiers entered his house. He was terrified, but he wouldn't run. He wanted to stand up to them as they invaded his house. So he stood and pointed right at them as he screamed. The background of the story is all too common. The Israeli military had assassinated several men in this village one week earlier, for being members of the resistance group. In response, a cousin of one of the men assassinated, blew himself up in Tel Aviv, killing a grandmother and a child. A few days later, the Israeli military invaded Balatta Refugee Camp, where the young man was from. It was a classic downward spiral of violence between the two sides of this conflict, each act a brutal response to the one that preceded it (Golan).

The invasion was predictably brutal. Homes were blown up. Curfew was imposed. Soldiers traveled through the cinderblock apartments these people called home, by taking sledgehammers to the walls. Without warning, in the middle of the night, you would simply hear the hammer crash and the sound of boots as soldiers marched through a hole in your wall. Observers on the ground report that this practice was so widespread, that the homes would often have arrows and directions spray painted on the walls, guiding the soldiers where they needed to go (Golan).

So perhaps it was strangely ironic that the boy was screaming as these soldiers came in through the front door. Perhaps he'd grown accustomed to the holes in the wall. Perhaps it was all this time trapped inside his home as heavily armed soldiers he was terrified of, walked in and out through the night. It might have been the sound of his neighbor's houses exploding as he wondered if his was next. The intermittent sound of gunfire could not have helped to calm him.

Neta and a few volunteers stayed with his family to help them deal with the invasion. This involved many things, all of them dangerous. Sometimes she broke curfew to walk injured people to the hospital, risking being shot herself for so doing. Sometimes it was something as simple as taking the children upstairs and teaching them a song, while the soldiers downstairs shattered the walls with a sledgehammer (Golan).

The boy was inconsolable as the soldiers entered the front door. He stood and pointed and screamed. He would not give ground. Even when his mother and the volunteers tried to move him to another room, he would not leave. One of the volunteers asked the soldier to remove his helmet, so the boy could see that he was human and not some monster from his nightmares. They had run into the soldier before and knew him to be reasonable. The soldier removed his helmet, and the boy calmed down a little. Then something extraordinary happened (Golan).

Even after all she had been through, the boy's mother did not want the boy to hate and fear all Israeli soldiers. She picked the boy up off the ground and told him to greet the soldier with a kiss. The boy obeyed his mother and kissed the soldier on the cheek. This soldier's uniform represented the people who had assassinated his neighbors only a few days before. It represented people who were now blowing up his other neighbors' homes. His mother who told him to do it had a million reasons to hate this soldier, but she didn't (Golan). This is the image that comes to my mind when I see the all too-frequent-TV news broadcasts showing the grief-stricken Palestinian mother calling for vengeance. It's become a tragic cliché. That image is designed to sell ad time not to illuminate the complex reality of this place.

Then, as if it was choreographed, the soldier returned the kiss of greeting to the boy and handed him a small Palestinian flag. The tender moment inevitably passed, and the family was herded into another room so the soldiers could search the place. The sound of furniture being destroyed could clearly be heard where they were. Neta taught the group a children's song to take their minds off of what was being done in the other room. The song worked its magic, and soon even the boy was singing and dancing to the song (Golan).

At this point, as Neta told the story, I was transfixed. However, I've been traveling to this region long enough to know that I didn't want to know the ending to the story. I didn't want to ask how it ended. I could live with the story where it was. But then I asked, "How did things end for the family?"

With a voice full of exhaustion born from seeing far too much, she said, "Soldiers came back at one o'clock in the morning and forced the grandmother to sing the children's song over and over at gunpoint" (Golan).

Any original connection the song had to childhood was no doubt shattered with the poor woman's command performance. Yet the same could be said for most things that we associate with childhood in this place. The Israeli occupation does not afford the people of the West Bank the luxury of a childhood. Children are born into a sea of pain as a birthright. Nearly a thousand Palestinian children were killed by Israeli Security Forces between September of 2000 and March of 2008, according to an Israeli human rights organization ("Trigger-Happy"). These numbers take on newfound severity when one considers the size of the population involved. The population of the United States is roughly 80 times larger than that of the West Bank and Gaza combined. So the proportional impact on the United States would be equivalent to 80,000 children being killed in a seven-and-one-half-year span.

✖ THE MAKING OF A SUICIDE BOMBER ✖

I was struck by something that Neta said after she told me the story. She was describing the Israeli military policy where all the men of Balata Refugee Camp were arrested and forcibly removed, before the soldiers went in to search the houses. They were moved into an overcrowded refugee camp a few miles away. This was probably close enough to be able to hear their homes being exploded and machine gun fire during curfew. Yet they were helpless to do anything to protect their families, as the worst possible scenario undoubtedly raced through their minds. She said, "I cannot think of a better way to make a proud Arab man into a terrorist"(Golan).

She spoke of how she often visited the Balata Refugee Camp. In these visits certain things became clear. She found it hard to believe that the Israeli military's actions were truly intended to quell violent Palestinian resistance. It seemed as if they were more intent on provoking resistance than ending it. It was clear to her that their actions made the situation so intolerable that resistance was the only option left open to the people of Balata.

She said that there had been no suicide bombers from the Camp until May of that year. In May, the Israeli military had assassinated two young men of the village which they accused of being members of the Palestinian resistance. While this may or may not have been true, the people of Balata saw members of the resistance as heroes because they defended the Camps from the Israeli military.

A camp that had not previously produced any suicide bombers suddenly produced seven of them in a matter of days after the young men were assassinated. These were not calculated, well-timed military strikes planned by ideological or religious zealots. These seven were young, poorly trained and angry. None of them had even seen their nineteenth birthdays. Several of them accidentally detonated their bombs on the way to their targets failing to achieve their goals. She told me these were clearly "acts of desperation." These were the type of acts that harsh military crackdowns tended to create rather than prevent.

She said there was only one thing that could prevent this. Give them hope. She gave an example. During the first intifada the Israeli Prime Minister Barak requested an end to the violent Palestinian resistance (bombing campaigns) in order to have peaceful elections. To give the Palestinian people hope that he would act in good faith; he lifted the siege and opened a few roadblocks that had been strangling the Occupied Territories. Hope bore fruit. The bombings stopped (Golan).

Is she right? I don't know. I've studied terrorism long enough to know that there are many different types of motivations that lead to suicide bombing. Hopelessness, misery, and revenge are powerful motivators. It is quite common for us as humans to lump all of the groups that use suicide bombing together in the same category. Yet this is far from true. Suicide bombing is a tactic, not a philosophy. Both Al Qaeda and some Palestinian resistance groups use suicide bombings to achieve their goals, but they're coming from very different starting points.

Al Qaeda is looking to restore a former Islamic empire from hundreds of years ago, that stretched from North Africa through the Middle East to Southeast Asia. Palestinian groups are trying to reclaim a tiny chunk of land that they or their fathers were born on. For Al Qaeda, it's an abstract goal. For the Palestinians, the goal, the pain, and the loss are deeply, deeply personal.

The Israeli invasion of Balata Refugee Camp was precipitated by a suicide bombing in Tel Aviv. The young man who committed that bombing, carefully and methodically collected all the fragments of the tank shell that the Israeli military had used to assassinate his cousin, and combined them with TNT to create his revenge. This is not a political act. This is not the act of a religious fanatic. This is infinitely personal.

This young man's cousin had been targeted by the Israeli military for assassination because he was a leader in a Palestinian resistance group. That resistance group had refrained from using tactics such as suicide bombing until early 2002. Why the change? Because in early 2002, Israeli military invaded Balata Refugee Camp and destroyed his home. When one is powerless to defend his own home and family, he changes tactics. It becomes personal. This is a pattern so often repeated that it makes one breathless trying to explain it.

I am reminded of comments made by a former Israeli soldier who became a member of Combatants for Peace. He described a pattern he saw emerging in the missions he was regularly sent on. He noticed a haunting connection between the names of the Palestinians who were killed or arrested during one of his missions, and the name of the Palestinian responsible for the next attack on Israel. It is a cycle of violence that is self-perpetuating. He came to the conclusion that the military solution was not working and that it never did.

These incredibly fertile breeding grounds like Balata that are constantly watered by hopelessness, pain, and grief, are beyond most Israelis' experience. The TV cameras very seldom show tanks daily roaming the streets of refugee camps like Balata, Jenin, or Rafah during a curfew period. Most Israeli journalists report from Jerusalem or Tel Aviv and rarely make it into the West Bank or Gaza. Palestinian reporters who have the courage to show this side of life, often find themselves to be the targets of Israeli soldiers. As a result, most Israelis don't see the conditions that breed the hopelessness that Neta talks about. They only see its natural fruition.

✂ BLACK HATS AND WHITE HATS ✂

For those people out there who like to cast the roles for this narrative with Henry Ford-like certainty (you know, you can have any color a car that you like, as long as it's black), here again is a story that defies stereotypes. Whether you think it was the noble Israeli military invading the village to get the big bad terrorists or it was the big bad Israeli military invading the noble village, there are some inconvenient facts. All of the activists with Neta (including herself) were Jewish. Some were Israeli, and some were internationals, but all were Jewish. Clearly they did not agree with Israeli government policy on this issue anymore than the Palestinian people of the village, and they were willing to put their lives on the line to demonstrate this.

The people of this village, who had every reason to fear Israelis, welcomed them into their homes with open arms and good humor. All this took place during a military curfew which put both parties at grave risk for their actions. The mother of the boy who had justification to hate and fear Israelis soldiers did neither, nor would she allow her boy to do so. The soldier who was supposed to follow orders and remain emotionally unattached, refused to renounce his humanity.

These are not the characters that we normally see in the blood-soaked news coverage of this region. Is this enough of a foundation upon which to build peace? I'm not sure, but at the very least, I think they are stories that need to be told.

✂ FEAR AND LOATHING IN TEL AVIV ✂

Why is it that the soldier who refused to renounce his humanity didn't take it a step further and refuse military service in the West Bank like so many others have done? Without speaking to the soldier in depth, we'll never really know, but I find some of the comments made by Neta in another context helpful:

My childhood was scary, and simple. There were good guys and bad guys. We were the good guys. The bad guys ... could be anyone, but they were mostly Arabs. Now I'm a third-generation Israeli: my grandmother was born in what was still called

Palestine. My mother was born in 1948. And yet, I grew up in the shadow of the Holocaust. It was always my reference point, for everything.

As a child, I met Palestinians. They were there, working in construction or sanitation. But there was never a chance to meet as equals. Instead there were fears, being fed by the media, by what we learned in school. I learned always that we were defending ourselves from people who wanted to kill us.

It wasn't until I was 15 years old that I learned of the occupation. It was during the first intifada, because before the first intifada, Palestinians, the occupation, simply didn't exist to us. The first intifada made it impossible for Israelis to ignore Palestinians. But I was raised on Jewish history, a history of oppression, dispossession, suffering ethnic cleansing, of being forced out of community after community. Ironically, the *whatever is necessary* position leads you to oppress, dispossess, and slaughter another group of victims.

Neta described her perspective when she was younger, this way:

I was part of the consensus opinion in Israel, that we are morally superior. They are violent. We have purity of arms. If we do kill a civilian or an innocent, it's by mistake. Even if these mistakes happen every single day, I didn't believe it until I saw it with my own eyes. I refused to believe that a soldier would open fire on an innocent child, but I saw it. Unfortunately in Nablus where I live, I see it too often. What I would hear about a child being killed by a soldier, I would think — no, he must've thrown a stone, he mustve been doing something that endangered the soldier and forced the soldier to shoot back. I wanted to believe that the children were throwing stones. But when you are in the West Bank, and you see a child throw a stone at a tank, you understand that if that child is killed, that is murder. And very recently, five internationals were with Baba, one of the children who we knew well, and soldiers in an armored personnel carrier picked

How can a soldier who feels genuine sympathy and tenderness toward a little boy screaming, crying, and pointing at him in a refugee camp, still see these people as his enemy? I describe this to my students as dual victimization. Both groups of people in this conflict have a legitimate right to view themselves as victims. One side in this conflict clearly has the monopoly on power. Under normal conditions, this might give one a sense of security. These are not normal conditions.

Being raised to believe that there are all sorts of people out there that want to kill you, changes your mindset. Being raised on stories of your ancestors being oppressed, dispossessed, and slaughtered prepares one to do whatever is necessary to avoid that for you and your community. Ironically, the *whatever is necessary* position leads you to oppress, dispossess, and slaughter another group of victims.

tation. But there was never a chance to meet as equals. Instead there were fears, being fed by the media, by what we learned in school. I learned always that we were defending ourselves from people who wanted to kill us.

sion, suffering ethnic cleansing, of being forced out of community after community. Could we really be doing these things to another people? (Rishmawi) *him out from among the internationals, shot him twice in the chest, and killed him (Rishmawi).*

Her fear of Palestinians was so deeply embedded that even after she started traveling to the West Bank to try to help them, she was afraid of them. During the Oslo peace process, she would travel to the West Bank with a deep anxiety in her chest, feeling that these Palestinians must want to kill her. To show how deep this runs, Neta at this time was engaged to be married to a man who was Palestinian. She confided in him her fears and asked if she was being paranoid. His response was, "yes!"

Keep in mind, this is not a woman who is easily frightened. She has been wounded in protests. She has snuck into cities under siege and walked people who needed medical attention to hospitals under curfew. And during all of this, she still manages to maintain a sense of humor. One of my favorite examples of this involves a protest over the destruction of an olive grove by the Israeli military.

These olive trees are not only important as a crop for Palestinians. There is often a deep symbolic importance as well. Much like some Palestinians whose claims on the land go back over a thousand years, olive trees in this part of the world can be thousands of years old, too. So you can imagine the rather unique connection as you tend a tree on your land all your life, that is the same olive tree that your great, great, great, great (you get the idea) grandfather tended.

Neta leads a protest to protect these trees from the Israeli Military bulldozer. It is an amazing scene. There is the normal intimidation and tear gas. Palestinian men are face down in the olive groves praying. And there is Neta with the chain around her neck that extends in both directions to connect to olive trees on either side. This places her directly in the path of the bulldozer. Five Israeli policemen approached her in an attempt to intimidate her. When this doesn't work, one finally asks, "What are you doing here?"

Neta responds with a straight face, "Your commander over there... the short bald guy. I have a crush on him in the worst way and if I don't do things like this... well, he just doesn't pay any attention to me." The policemen try unsuccessfully not to laugh. All this was taking place as the bulldozer shovel was raised menacingly over her head (Golan).

As I stated earlier, Neta is not the type of person to be frightened easily. However, when someone as strong as her admits to having anxiety when walking among Palestinians in the West Bank, that gives one an idea of how deeply impacting this culture of fear and victimization can be. The following ironic story provides a good example of my point.

Neta was traveling by bus back home to see her parents to celebrate the Passover Seder. I can think of few events that are more pivotal in both the Jewish and Israeli identity as Passover. Here is a Jewish Israeli woman on her way home to celebrate this event with her parents. During the bus ride, she receives a phone call. It has to do with a protest that she's planning but will not be able to attend because she's celebrating Passover. An Israeli woman sitting near her on the bus hears the conversation and immediately calls the Israeli police.

The bus is stopped by the Israeli police, and Neta is taken into custody. As it became clear that the police were going to stop the bus, the woman sitting near Neta informed her that she had called the police. Neta looked at her in amazement and asked, "Are you worried that I'm carrying a bomb or something? Why would you have me arrested for talking on the phone about a legal protest?"

The woman responded, "Of course, I know you don't have a bomb. But you are a collaborator" (Golan).

To this woman, as well as many other Israelis I have spoken with, the perfectly legal, non-violent type of protest that Neta engages in, is the equivalent of treason. To disagree with Israeli government policies regarding the Palestinians, is to collaborate with the enemy whether that policy is right or wrong. The deep and abiding fear that produces an attitude like this is quite prevalent in Israeli society.

Palestinians live in fear as well, but it's a bit different. Israelis worry about when the next action by their enemy will bring pain into their life. Most Palestinians don't have to wonder. It's remarkably consistent. It's the checkpoint, the tear gas, the steel bullets with rubber coating. For others, it is tank shells and rocket fire from helicopter gunships.

Beyond the obvious wounds that attacks like these create, there are ones that are harder to see. Simply witnessing violence on a regular basis causes damage that cannot simply be stitched up in a hospital. According to a study at Queens University, 98% of Gaza's children experience or witness war trauma (Science Daily).

Neta chooses to live in the midst of this conflict in an attempt to make a difference. In one sense, she has less choice than it may appear. Her husband is Palestinian. She jokes that they are *illegal as a unit.* According to Israeli law, she cannot live in the West Bank as an Israeli citizen. According to that same law, he cannot live in Israel as a Palestinian. So she chooses to stay with her husband and raise her two children Nawal and Shaden in the West Bank. I will end with a tragically beautiful comment that she made once:

"Back home in Nablus, Nawal and myself came back to our family and to the routine of waking up every night from the explosion of homes being destroyed, or tanks thundering through the streets and shooting. In the meantime, Nawal has learned to smile and, when she smiles, she shines like the sun" (Golan; Golan "The Long Journey").

✄ THE WAY I DIDN'T WANT TO END THIS CHAPTER ✄

I really wanted to end the chapter with that beautiful quote. It was such an elegant mixture of the tragic and the hopeful. Perhaps it's a function of the place about which I write, that one cannot end a story with a smiling child. Neta has made many sacrifices in her work with the International Solidarity Movement. Yet, I can't, in good conscience, end the chapter about the International Solidarity Movement without mentioning some of those who've made the ultimate sacrifice.

She was a compassionate young woman who was driven to help those in need. She worked to feed the hungry. She helped the homeless. Today, she stood in front of a friend's home opposing an Israeli military bulldozer. She was a poet, a college student, and an American. Her friend who lived in the home about to be demolished, was a Palestinian doctor. She wore a bright fluorescent orange vest and pleaded with the driver of the bulldozer to stop, through her megaphone.

But he crushed her – not once, but twice. After he ran her over the first time, he backed the 157, 849 pound vehicle over her again (assuming it was a D9 Bulldozer which is 71.6 metric tons) as other peace activists stood by helplessly and watched. The Israeli military later claimed that the driver did not see her. Yet, this dynamic of peace activists standing in front of a home was not a new one. It had been going on for some time. In fact, in the month previous to Rachel's death, international peace activists had attempted to prevent the destruction of homes and water sources in this way on February 11, 12, 14, 21, 23, and 24. The activists made sure they were not difficult to see. They generally carried large banners, carried megaphones, and wore bright orange vests.

Nor was this dynamic new to Rachel. She had been present at the February 14 demonstration. Rachel and six other internationals had responded to a report of a house demolition. When arriving on the scene, they encountered two bulldozers and a tank. As the activists stood in the path of the bulldozer to prevent it from demolishing a house, a driver raised the blade of the shovel toward them. They did not move. The driver then physically struck them with a shovel, pushing them backwards. At this point, Rachel and the other activists were forced to take shelter inside the home they were trying to save. This did not discourage the driver of the bulldozer.

He smashed through the wall of the house. After smashing through the wall, he threw concussion grenades inside and continued to demolish the rest of the house. Rachel and six other activists were forced to flee amid gunfire from the tank. They were not able to save this house ("Israeli Bulldozer Kills American Woman;" Kapitan; Let Me Stand Alone).

Perhaps the day that Rachel died, the driver didn't see her. Eye witness accounts say he clearly did. Yet, in one sense, I'm not sure that it matters. It's rather clear that the orders the bulldozer and tank drivers were operating under were not concerned with safeguarding human life, whether Palestinian or American. With the number of house demolitions, if it wasn't this Rachel, it would have been another Rachel who died eventually.

Other International Solidarity Movement peace activists like Rachel have paid the ultimate price. We hear very little about it in the mainstream American press. Thomas Hurndall, a 22-year-old British peace activist, attempted to protect a few Palestinian children caught in crossfire. While shielding the child from the gunfire and wearing his fluorescent orange vest, Tom was shot in the head by an Israeli sniper. Originally, he and some other peace activists were going to set up a peace tent to protest Israeli military invasion of Rafah. However, as the Israeli tanks rolled in, Palestinian gunmen returned fire. The activists moved out of the crossfire, but a group of children were still trapped there. Some ran, but others were paralyzed by fear. Tom was able to rescue one little girl, but then he ran back for another. As he knelt down next to the child, the sniper found his target (Atkinson).

I struggle to think of anything more noteworthy to have on your tombstone than the phrase, "amid gunfire, he ran back for *another* child."

CHAPTER 8

Just Another Day in the South Hebron Hills

Nine frightened children approach Little Rock Central High School, accompanied by soldiers. A group of people around them scream racial insults and threaten them. They were black and the school was white. This was their only crime.

This was not their first time. The first time was even worse. As Elizabeth Eckford approached the school, the crowd shouted, "Lynch her! Lynch her!" Her knees started to shake. "Go back where you came from!" screamed someone from the crowd. The crowd was now all around her. She frantically looked for some friendly face. She saw an older woman who looked friendly as she scanned the crowd. As Elizabeth turned her head back and looked at the old woman for support, the woman spat at her.

Elizabeth retreated through the crowd and back to an empty bench at the bus stop away from the school. Some of the crowd followed her. A voice from the crowd shouted, "Drag her over to this tree!" A few of the reporters present formed a circle around her, attempting to provide a little protection. One white reporter did the unthinkable. He sat down next to her on the bench and put his arm around her. He then lifted her chin with his and said, "Don't let them see you cry."

The husband of Daisy Bates, who had organized the Little Rock Nine, offered to walk Elizabeth home. He showed her that he was carrying a gun. Elizabeth declined, knowing that her mother would not approve of her walking home with strange man. Ultimately, it was a white woman who helped Elizabeth get away from the mob. Grace Lorch told the crowd that one day they would be ashamed of themselves, as she escorted Elizabeth onto the bus that would take her home (Vanity Fair).

As we discuss stories like this in my American history class, it's always a relief to note that situations like this generally don't occur in America anymore. Yet they still do occur. Each day, Palestinian children in the South Hebron Hills walk with their reluctant Israeli military escort to school. I say reluctant because the soldiers that escort them, often only walk part of the way to and from school and then stop, thus abandoning them in an area where mobs of angry Israeli settlers from an illegal settlement have attacked them in the past (Christian Peacemaker Teams).

In January of 2008, the soldiers began refusing to come to the assigned meeting place to escort the children. They would stop a good distance off, thus forcing the children to walk to them, through the territory where they had been attacked previously. The children in this group ranged in age from six years old to eleven years old. In one incident, a large man from the illegal settlement approached the children, yelling threats with a stone in his hand. The children looked at the soldiers who were under orders to protect them. The settler was apparently not very concerned about the soldiers, as he was seen chatting with them off and on during this incident (Palestinian News Network).

These incidents are not uncommon. Later that same month, masked settlers drove through the village, shouting insults and throwing stones at Palestinian children, as well as a woman carrying a baby. The following morning, Palestinian children on their way to school were attacked by a group of settlers throwing stones (The Mennonite). In fact, the presence of Israeli soldiers as military escorts for the children dates back to similar incidents in 2004.

Two American members of the Christian Peacemaker Teams were escorting the children to school. This had been the practice of the Christian Peacemaker Teams since the attacks on the children had started, long before pressure on the Israeli government forced them to send soldiers to escort the children. Christian Peacemaker Teams lend a hand to vulnerable people all over the world in this way.

Chris Brown, an African-American man from San Francisco, saw five men approach wearing masks. They carried bats, chains, and rocks. This wasn't the first time that Chris had faced men filled with hate. Chris was born and spent the first eight years of his life in South Africa during apartheid. As an adult, he would have the courage to return to South Africa and struggle against apartheid. The price of his commitment was spending a year and a half in jail. Most of this time was spent in solitary confinement.

As the masked men approached, Chris's primary concern was for the children. He jumped in front of the children and yelled, "Please don't hurt the children." One of the men slammed a large rock against the side of his head. Chris crumpled to the ground. At this point, the men began beating him with baseball bats and chains on the ground and kicking him with their steel-toed boots. Chris cried out, "Why are you doing this? All we're doing is walking children to school. We're nonviolent. We are Americans." At this point one of the masked men laughed and said, "They're Americans."

Chris's fellow American, Kim Lamberry, was being beaten as well. She lay facedown on the ground, not moving as the masked men kicked and beat her. She describes much of the attack as a blur. She simply hoped that if she laid there and pretended she was unconscious, they might leave her alone. When the men had finished beating the two American peacemakers, they stole Kim's money, passport, and cell phone. After the men finally left, Kim crawled over to Chris's body to find his cell phone and call for help. She couldn't walk.

She called two other members of Christian Peacemaker Teams in the area. They quickly ran through the same dangerous territory, knowing full well that they could be attacked and beaten just like Chris and Kim. The Israeli ambulance, which arrived long after it had been called, took the two peacemakers to the hospital. Chris had a punctured lung and broken ribs, in addition to the cuts and contusions that covered his whole body. Kim had contusions over her whole body as well. In addition, the attackers had severely damaged her knee and broken her arm. Due to this sacrificial act on the part of peacemakers, the children were able to flee back to the village (Weir).

Long before the Palestinian/Israeli conflict raged in the Middle East, the United States was dealing with its own form of ethnic conflict, a conflict that some of our most legendary minds viewed as unsolvable.

> It will probably be asked, why not retain and incorporate the blacks into the state, and thus save the expense of supplying, by importation of white settlers, the vacancies they will leave? Deep-rooted prejudices entertained by the whites; ten thousand recollections, by the blacks, of the injuries they have sustained; new provocations; the real distinctions which nature has made; and many other circumstances, will divide us into parties, and produce convulsions, which will probably never end but in the extermination of one or the other race (Jefferson).

Yet we did not exterminate each other. Thomas Jefferson, who penned the words above, had a brilliant mind, but he was wrong. Many other important people of the time agreed with Jefferson that the races were incompatible. They were wrong as well. Not only have we, as a united people, come a long way from slavery, but we've come a long way from the days of the Jim Crow South as well.

It is not impossible, even though it may have seemed so at the time. Peace between the Israelis and the Palestinians appears impossible today. Yet I do not believe that it is impossible. People frequently tell me that they've always been fighting over there, and they always will be. It is indeed true that they've been fighting for about 80 to 90 years. This is not thousands of years as the above statement implies, yet it is indeed a long time. However, American slavery lasted for several centuries. Today, it no longer exists.

People will often tell me that there's too much hate to overcome after all the bloodshed over there. However, even a cursory look at the bloodshed and brutality of both the slavery period and the Jim Crow period, challenges the notion that people are trapped permanently in their own history. In fact, one of the only constants in history, is change. People suggested that the Irish would always be fighting the British government, but that's no longer the case. People suggested that women would never obtain the right to vote. Yet today not only do women vote, but as I write these words in the 2008 election season, a woman named, Hillary Clinton, has a reasonable chance of becoming our next president.

Will it be difficult? Yes, but it was difficult then as well. It will require sacrifice. Look at the story of the Little Rock Nine. It was a white reporter from the north, an outsider, who had the courage to sit next to Elizabeth Eckford as the mob swirled around both of them. Members of the Christian Peacemaker Teams, outsiders from all over the world, regularly stand up to mobs in the West Bank.

Perhaps even more courageous than the white reporter from the north was Grace Lorch, a white woman married to a local college professor. Grace stood between the mob and Elizabeth, not only protecting Elizabeth, but at the same time chastising the mob and telling them they would be ashamed of their behavior one day. Keep in mind, Grace had to live in this community after her actions. She was not an outsider. She lived there. Although she was part of the ethnic group that held all the power, she still chose to challenge it.

The price of her actions was high. Her husband was forced out of his job at the local college. Her daughter was beaten at school. Grace was summoned before the Senate Internal Security Subcommittee. Dynamite was placed under the family's garage door (State University of New York at Buffalo).

Today, many Israelis come to the South Hebron Hills to help and stand in solidarity with the Christian Peacemaker Teams. When I interviewed Sally Hunsberger, a member of the Christian Peacemaker Teams who had served in that area, she described an event where she saw two busloads of Israelis, disembark and meet with local impoverished Palestinians who were suffering due to new Israeli settlements in the area. Like Grace Lorch, they are part of the ethnic group that holds all the power and yet they choose to challenge it. It is illegal, according to the Israeli government, for these Israeli citizens to even be in the West Bank.

Just as the civil rights struggle in the United States required sacrifice from people other than the African-Americans trapped in the situation, for the Palestinian-Israeli conflict, it will require sacrifice on the part of both outsiders and Israelis. The sad truth is that sacrifice on the part of these two groups tends to get far more attention from the world than sacrifice on the part of the Palestinians. The good news is there are both outsiders and Israelis with the courage to sacrifice. Israeli human rights groups such as Rabbis for Human Rights and Ta'ayush have regularly traveled to the South Hebron Hills to help the Palestinians that live there. Outsiders such as Christian Peacemaker Teams and Operation Dove maintain a constant presence there year-round.

Peace between the Palestinians and Israelis may indeed take a long time, as some suggest. Yet changes of this sort can happen remarkably fast sometimes. Returning to the history of the Little Rock Nine, there is an important character I have not mentioned yet. Her name is Hazel Brown. Hazel became the poster child for hate when she was photographed screaming at Elizabeth Eckford on that fateful day in Little Rock, Arkansas. The photograph ranks among the most famous of the 20th century. Every American history textbook I've taught from over the last 15 years has had this photo in it.

Over the years, Hazel's views on race evolved with those of the rest of the country. Six years later, she called Elizabeth to apologize for her behavior. Hazel went on to challenge the racial views of her Church and was ultimately kicked out. Later she would work with young African-

American mothers-to-be as well as counseling other minority students. Ultimately, 40 years later at the anniversary of the event in Little Rock, Hazel and Elizabeth came together again in front of the high school. By now, the two women had become friends. A new photograph of the two women together was taken. Hazel had now moved from the poster child for hate to the poster child for reconciliation.

I sometimes think about the statement made by Grace Lorch back in 1957. She told the crowd that one day they would be ashamed of their actions. As citizens of the most powerful country in the world, which regularly supports Israeli policy that results in tragedy for the Palestinians, will we be ashamed 50 years from now?

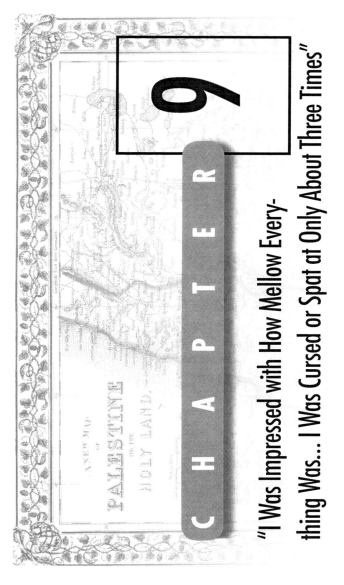

CHAPTER 9

"I Was Impressed with How Mellow Everything Was... I Was Cursed or Spat at Only About Three Times"

❧ **THE FACE OF HEBRON** ❧

"I'll be the 68-year-old man with a white beard and a red hat standing at Babia Zohia." And so he was. His clothes were worn and tattered. His smile was radiant and contagious. He stood on the streets of Hebron, arguably one of the most contentious and deadly areas of the Palestinian-Israeli conflict, this 68-year-old Ohio farmer. One could say it was surreal, but in a larger sense, it wasn't. Although the man looked every inch an American from his red CPT baseball cap to his weathered tennis shoes, he looked perfectly at home in this large, contentious, Middle Eastern city as its Palestinian residents swirled around him.

We had spoken many times via e-mail but never spoken in person. I was bringing a group of Americans to meet this remarkable man and to let him show them the realities of this troubled place. I jumped off the minibus and went over to meet him. His first words were, "Hmm, I thought you'd be older." I said, "Yeah, I get that a lot." I waved to my group that it was okay to get off the bus. I needed to balance the safety of the group with the importance of letting the bus leave as quickly as possible. A Palestinian driver stopped for too long, could bring unwanted attention from the Israeli military. This could result in serious trouble for him. So I waved to Uncle Sam, my favorite driver in the West Bank, and he pulled away with his ubiquitous wry grin.

As I turned back towards the bearded 68-year-old Ohio farmer, he addressed my group and said, "Well, you have just completed the most dangerous part of the time you will spend here." As everyone looked at him blankly, he said, "Your drive over here, I mean." And then he smiled that disarming smile of his.

The word, disarming, is key here. This man has faced armed people all too often in his 13 years traveling to this place, and one of his most effective weapons has been that smile. This is true of many of the people that do what he does. His name is Art Gish, and he's a member of the Christian Peacemaker Teams. These days he spends most of his time south of Hebron in a small village called At-Tuwani. This is the area in which Chris Brown and Kim Lamberty were beaten by the settlers for walking children to school. This is what Art Gish does everyday.

Before Art moved to At-Tuwani, he spent most of his time in Hebron. The city is home to 166,000 Palestinians. In 1968, the first group of Jewish settlers to move to the West Bank moved into the center of Hebron. The group was led by Moshe Levinger, a Zionist rabbi. The group rented rooms at a hotel in downtown Hebron and then refused to leave. They then announced their intent to establish a settlement for Jews only in Hebron. With the support of the Israeli government, they were able to do so, and the settlement of Kiryat Arba was born. As time went on, more Israeli settlers established settlements in the same way.

The result today is that the lives of 166,000 Palestinians are controlled by an Israeli military force of approximately 150,000 soldiers. The soldiers are there to protect Moshe Levinger and his followers, who still live in the center of the city. Their exact numbers are up to debate. I've heard numbers as low as a hundred, and many of the settlers claim 600. Either way the city is paralyzed by their presence.

❧ AN ATTACK ON PEACE AND JUSTICE ❧

CPT was invited to maintain a presence in Hebron in 1995 by the Palestinian mayor, to help reverse the escalation in violence between the Israeli soldiers, settlers, and the Palestinians. Between 1994 and 1996, soldiers and settlers killed 70 Palestinians. In response, Palestinians killed several Israelis. One of the most famous events happened in February of 1994 when Baruch Goldstein, an Israeli settler from the Kiryat Arba settlement, walked into a mosque in Hebron and fired his machine gun into Palestinian worshipers as they prayed. He was able to kill 29 people and wound another 150 before he had to reload his weapon. While he was reloading for another attempt, he was tackled and killed by the survivors. In the demonstrations following the massacre, Israeli soldiers shot and killed 26 more Palestinians. A curfew was imposed for 40 days, restricting all movement. Ironically, the curfew was only enforced on the Palestinians of Hebron. The settlers were free to move around at will (Gish 25).

This was the political landscape of Hebron when Art Gish showed up in 1995. Simple things in life become quite difficult under these conditions. One of the first acts by the Christian Peacemaker Teams in Hebron was to make sure Palestinians were given access to water, which had been denied. As more and more settlers moved into the area and developed illegal settlements on Palestinian land, problems developed. When the regular municipal water trucks transported water to Palestinian farmers, the settlers living nearby would smash the windshields of the trucks. Thus regular water delivery stopped. Christian Peacemaker Team members started accompanying the trucks. Eventually, they were detained by Israeli police for doing this. This detention brought international attention to the problem in Hebron. Israeli citizens who had never been to Hebron wanted to understand why the Israeli settlements right next the Palestinian farmers had plenty of water while the Palestinians went without ("Chronology").

That was 1995 when CPT first arrived in Hebron. These types of struggles continue today. In April of this year, the Israeli military raided an all-girl orphanage. The irony was not lost on most Palestinians in the area, that the orphanage was located on the corner of Peace and Justice streets. CPT was able to video tape the 40 Israeli soldiers stealing $45,000 worth of sewing machines, office equipment, finished clothing, rolls of fabric, etc. One CPT worker was quoted as saying, "How can grown men do this to little children?" ("Joy Ellison Blog").

A bittersweet gift that technology has given the world is the ability to document incidents such as this. The Israeli human rights group B'Tselem has started a new project with this in mind. Its darkly humorous title is "shooting back." The project was launched in January 2007 by providing Palestinians in the West Bank who lived near settlements or military bases, with video cameras. The purpose was to give Palestinians the ability to document the extraordinary human rights abuses that they endure regularly. B'Tselem has been able to air this video footage on major Israeli and international news networks, giving global audiences the chance to see the daily reality that is normally kept hidden.

You can see an elderly Palestinian couple shepherding their flock in the fields while four young masked settlers approach with baseball bats. The elderly shepherd approaches them with open hands in a gesture of peace. You watch as the baseball bat falls upon him again and again. You watch a woman in Hebron scream for help to a soldier as settlers prevent her brother from being able to come into the house. The soldier tells her to shut up and go inside, while a settler woman inches from her face tells her that she's a whore and that her daughters are whores again and again. Anyone can download this footage at their website where it's archived. You can see an attack on a family in the South Hebron Hills by settlers. The son desperately tries to hold the camera still while running backwards from his attackers. You can hear his mother scream.

✂ "EVERY FAMILY SHOULD HAVE A HOME." ✂

Yet, the picture I've just painted of Hebron is too simplistic. Inside this cycle of revenge between Palestinians and the Israeli settlers and soldiers is a complexity often overlooked. In an interview I conducted with Kathy Kamphoefner, she told a story that powerfully illustrates this complexity. Kathy is a member of CPT who was present in the early days of the Hebron CPT office and has been continually involved in nonviolence through today.

During her time with CPT in Hebron, she would attempt to engage the settlers in dialogue to better understand their position on the conflict. During one of these encounters, she had dinner with a settler couple named Sam and Miriam in Kiryat Arba. As they enjoyed home-made ice cream following dinner, Sam told Kathy that she was being too nice and that she could ask the tough questions if she wanted to. From here, the conversation grew more frank and honest but also more intense. As they discussed violence committed by both sides, Kathy cited the recent death tolls for both Israelis and Palestinians.

Sam was shocked by the numbers. It wasn't the magnitude of the numbers but their distribution that surprised him. He had always been informed that the settlers were more often the victims of violence. As it turned out, the death tolls that Kathy cited showed that far more Palestinians were being killed by Israelis than visa versa. This has consistently been the case throughout the conflict. For example, current numbers for the second Intifada (since 2000) illustrate that over nine times as many Palestinian children have been killed as compared to Israeli children (B'Tselem Website, 2008).

What is interesting here is that Sam is an intelligent, well-educated man. Why would a man like this believe something so far from the truth? Most Israelis are insulated from the daily brutality of events in the West Bank because they live in Israel proper, and the Israeli government has declared it illegal for its citizens to travel in the West Bank. Yet, Sam lives in the West Bank. But does he really live in the West Bank?

Most of the settlers live in insulated bubbles of their own, attached by an umbilical cord to Israel proper. These settlements are housing developments in the West Bank generally built on the best Palestinian land and reserved for Jewish inhabitants only. I use the word, Jewish, here because there are Palestinians who have Israeli citizenship but still cannot live in one of these. They are protected by the Israeli military or armed Israeli settlers, or frequently both. They are connected to Israel proper by roads built for use only by Israeli settlers. The Palestinians refer to these as "Apartheid Roads" due to the race-based criteria for their use.

The following description of the settlement situation from the Palestine Monitor will give the reader a snapshot of the situation:

> There are currently 120 Israeli settlements and 102 Israeli outposts built illegally in the West Bank including East Jerusalem, which is Palestinian land occupied by Israel in 1967. All of these settlements and outposts are illegal under international law and numerous United Nations Security Council resolutions. Israeli outposts are also illegal under Israeli law...due to the extensive network of settler roads and restrictions on Palestinians accessing their own land, Israeli settlements dominate more than 40 percent of the West Bank.

> Settlements are linked to each other and to Israel by an extensive network of bypass roads. For each 100 km of bypass road, about 2,500 acres of West Bank land is confiscated. All bypass roads have a 50-75m buffer zone on each side, where no construction is allowed. These buffer zones have led to a great loss of agricultural and privately-owned Palestinian land.

Whilst illegally built on confiscated Palestinian land, these roads are forbidden for use by Palestinians. They consolidate Israel's creation of a system of apartheid in the West Bank, and fracture communities across Palestine.

Settlements are the cause of great inequalities in access to natural resources between Israelis and Palestinians. Many settlements are built on prime agricultural land confiscated from Palestinians, or over key water resources such as the Western Aquifer basin, springs, and wells. This has resulted in Israeli West Bank settlers being allocated 2400 m3 of water per year compared to 50 m3 for Palestinians. Such inequalities are being consolidated by the Wall, which will annex swathes of Palestinian agricultural land and major vital water resources to Israel.

The route of Israel's Wall has been designed to annex 56 settlements to Israel, incorporating 76 percent of the settler population currently living in the West Bank (including settlements in East Jerusalem).

The Wall and Israel's matrix of settlements will sever the West Bank into 4 cantons, fracturing its geographic, political, economic, and social cohesion and totally undermining the possibility of a future, contiguous and independent Palestinian state.

Kathy's conversation with Sam shifted from death tolls to housing demolitions. The Israeli Committee Against House Demolitions describes the situations this way:

Since 1967, 18,000 Palestinian homes have been demolished in the Occupied Territories, including East Jerusalem. Almost 1,700 Palestinian homes in the Occupied Territories were demolished by the Civil Administration during the course of the Oslo peace process (1993-2000). Since the start of the second Intifada in September 2000, about 5000 Palestinian homes have been destroyed in military operations, including hundreds in Jenin, Nablus, Ramallah, Bethlehem, Hebron, and other cities of the West Bank, more than 2500 in Gaza alone. Tens of thousands of other homes have been left uninhabitable. Altogether around 50,000 people have been left homeless (Human Rights Watch, Razing Rafah, October 2004). Hundreds of shops, workshops, factories, and public buildings, including all the Palestinian Authority ministry offices in all the West Bank cities, have also been destroyed or damaged beyond repair. According to Amnesty International more than 3000 hectares of cultivated land – 10% of the agricultural land of Gaza – have been cleared during this time. Wells, water storage pools, and water pumps which provided water for drinking, irrigation, and other needs for thousands of people, have also been destroyed, along with tens of kilometers of irriga-

tion networks. More than 628 Palestinian homes have been demolished during the second Intifada as collective punishment and deterrence affecting families of people known or suspected of involvement in attacks on Israeli civilians. On average, 12 innocent people lose their home for every person punished for a security offense – and in half of the cases the occupants had nothing whatsoever to do with the acts in question. To add to the Kafkaesque nature of this policy, the Israeli government insists its aim is to deter potential terrorists, although 79% of the suspected offenders were either dead or in detention at the time of the demolition (B'tselem Summary 2004:1,3). Israel's policy of house demolitions seeks to confine Palestinians to small enclaves, leaving most of the land free for Israeli settlement (Israeli Committee Against Housing Demolitions).

However, it was not the statistics that moved Sam. It was a story that Kathy told of a recent event that took place nearby, to a family that CPT had been helping. Approximately one hour after a CPT member had left the family's home, a large group of Israeli soldiers and police came to the Al Atrash family's home. The family was rebuilding from the last time the Israeli military demolished it on March 3, 1998.

Two CPT workers returned to the home after receiving a call for help. When they arrived, they found their 14-year-old daughter taking care of her seven younger brothers and sisters. She explained that the soldiers had hit her parents as well as herself and her three-year-old brother, Mazen Dana, a Reuters journalist present at the time, said, "It was disgusting. They were dragging the mother around on the ground by her hair and beating her with the ends of their rifles. They tore her dress and showed her breasts." Footage of the mother being dragged by soldiers appeared on Israeli television. Four members of the family were arrested (Christian Peacemaker Teams "News Archive").

About a week later, a similar scene was played out again when soldiers arrived to confiscate a cement mixer that the family had been using to rebuild their home. Mother and daughter were kicked and punched by Israeli soldiers while they were handcuffed on the ground. Gideon Levy, an Israeli journalist, witnessed the events. After her release from jail, the mother needed medical attention three times, twice for coughing up blood and abdominal pain and once for losing consciousness after a severe headache.

The reactions of Sam and Miriam could not have been more different. Sam was speechless. Miriam refused to believe the story was true even though it had been covered on the Israeli news. As the conversation wound down, Kathy rose to leave. Miriam went to the kitchen, not desiring to wish Kathy a good evening. Sam walked her to the door. As they said goodbye, Sam quickly thrust some money into Kathy's hand. "Every family deserves a home," he said.

The next time Kathy saw Sam again, he was not in Hebron. He was in Jerusalem. Miriam was not with him. They had since separated. He was rebuilding a Palestinian family's home that had been destroyed by the Israeli Military. At the time of this writing, this house has been demolished four times and built for the fifth time.

It is easy to generalize about the way all Palestinians and Israelis feel about each other. It is even easier when you are discussing a particular group, such as Israeli settlers. Yet Sam and Miriam clearly demonstrate that even within a community of settlers, there are differing views, particularly when they are confronted by accurate information about the conflict of which they are a part. There was something inside Sam and Miriam that caused one to challenge the misinformation he'd been led to believe, and the other to dive even deeper into the pool of misinformation. Yet would either one of them have challenged their own propaganda had they not been challenged by a CPT member? Art provided me with another example of this while walking around Hebron one day.

✖ HE HAD A RAZOR TO HIS THROAT ✖

As Art led me and my group around Hebron, the reputation this city had for being one of the epicenters for the hatred produced by the Palestinian-Israeli conflict, was both confirmed and challenged. As we passed a pile of stone rubble that had recently been a Palestinian family's home, Art pointed to a house on the hill in the distance. This home, which had once been all alone on that hillside, now looked as if it was about to be crushed by this Israeli settlement on the top of the hill. As I looked at the settlement, it looked like a living, breathing entity slowly crawling down the hill to swallow the small home.

As it turns out, my analogy was tragically accurate. Settlers had recently been throwing stones at the windows of the home and attacking the family members when they came outside. If the family gave in to the pressure and left the house, it would make it easy for the settlers to take the land. If they stayed, it could end up being their tomb. Art was pointing this out because settlers had recently broken into the house and attacked the family. Dozens of settlers hurled stones, empty bottles, and iron bars at the home after their prayer session the day before. The barrage resulted in injuries of 11 family members, including four children. Several of them suffered from concussions when they were hit in the head with rocks and other objects (Bannoura).

According to eyewitnesses, when Israeli soldiers arrived on the scene, they fired tear gas bombs inside the house, further endangering and injuring the family members. Eyewitnesses reported that both settlers and soldiers participated in the attack, and when the family members tried to fend off the attack by holding up their hands, they were beaten down. The soldiers surrounded the home and prevented medics from entering to bring the injured to the hospital (Bannoura). As a result, a CPT member had agreed to spend the night with the family for protection or perhaps, as is too often the case, just to witness the tragic events that might unfold.

As we walked away from the house on the hill, we passed the rubble of the former Palestinian home, and I noticed some children playing among the stones. As an Israeli military vehicle raced passed us on the street, I saw one of the children pick up a stone and hurl it ineffectually towards the vehicle. I asked Art if he knew who those children were. "Yes," he said. "They used to live in that house."

We proceeded on down the hill, and suddenly a man turned quickly toward Art. He was an Israeli settler. The memory that settlers had assaulted Art in the past, not to mention threatened his life, flashed through my head. Before I knew it, the two men grabbed hold of each other. They were hugging. This really shouldn't have surprised me. Though many of the settlers hated CPT, and Art in particular, for standing between them and their intended targets, the Palestinians, Art had always worked hard and risked his life to try and establish relationships with these people.

The two men turned toward us with broad smiles, and Art introduced us to Arnold. Arnold was indeed a settler from Kiryat Arba, but he did not adopt all of the common views of the settlers there. First and foremost, he did not despise Art in the way that many of the others clearly did. He respected Art's persistence in establishing some sort of positive relationship with the settlers of Kiryat Arba. He realized that Art persisted in spite of the fact that he'd been assaulted and threatened by these settlers again and again.

In fact, Arnold risked a potential backlash against himself by openly hugging this man that many of his neighbors viewed as an enemy. This was one of the many things that I found charming about Arnold. In many ways, he was able to rise above the simplistic vision of his community and see reality as a more complex beast to be grappled with. As we walked away from Arnold, Art told a story that exemplified this. With the evocative look of a great storyteller, he turned to the group and said, "You know Arnold once had a Palestinian hold a razor to his throat."

He let his words resonate for a moment. They had the intended effect. As I looked around the group, it was clear he'd captured them. Everyone was waiting for his next word. "Yep. The other day he went in for a haircut and a shave from a Palestinian barber." As he completed the sentence, a broad grin stretched across his face. One by one people in the group realized that what he was describing was just a normal haircut and shave. Yet, while this is technically true, is any interaction involving a Palestinian holding a straight razor against the throat of a settler from Kiryat Arba, one of the most consistently violent settler groups, truly a normal circumstance?

Do incidents like this suggest that there can be peace one day in this land? Art seems to think so. Some would dismiss this as a utopian vision. Yet, most of those who would dismiss this idea don't have anywhere close to as much on-the-ground experience with this conflict as Art does. In reality, very few Washington DC policymakers do either. In my humble opinion, spending all your time in Jerusalem or Tel Aviv doesn't really count.

All this being said, Arnold agreed with many of the settlers that there was little chance for peace with the Palestinians. His has a more complexly negative view than that of his neighbors. His disdain was for the Palestinian leadership, not necessarily the Palestinian people. Like many of us, he was wonderfully inconsistent and all-too-human. Maybe that's why I liked him so much.

❦ THIS WORK OF ART ❧

Art first met Arnold as part of his constant effort to establish a rapport with the settler community. Not all of them were as receptive as Arnold. Art was consistently threatened with death by the settlers. Sometimes they were explicit, such as stating, "I will kill you," or "We can kill you," as they walked by. Sometimes it was more subtle, like when they would simply drag their finger across their throat like a knife as they glared at him (Gish).

They seemed to hate him for two reasons. The first reason was based upon perception and the second upon reality. Let's deal with the perception first. The settler perception of CPT in general and Art in particular, is that they are partisans on the Palestinian side and thus against the settlers. Art answers this misperception effectively when he says, "We stand on the side of whomever the gun is pointed at, whoever is suffering injustice. We engage in the conflict, not as objective observers, but by standing in the middle" (Gish).

The on-the-ground reality is that the Israeli soldiers and settlers possess an overwhelming majority of the guns. As a result, they are much more likely to have the power to point them at the Palestinians than the Palestinians are to point guns toward them. So the CPT philosophy combined with the realities on-the-ground, gives the perception that CPT stands with the Palestinians all the time. Yet, when the Palestinians have had the weapons and have pointed them, CPT has shown a willingness to stand in the way.

In 1996, Hamas blew up the #18 bus in Jerusalem twice. The following Sunday, CPT members chose to ride the #18 bus in Jerusalem from six to nine in the morning. They alerted the Arab, Israeli, and international press before they rode the bus, to make it clear that this was a nonviolent protest against the bombings. The morning passed without incident.

The hatred that many of the settlers felt toward Art was also based, in part, on the reality of his actions. As we walked through Hebron's central market area, I watched again and again as Palestinians walked up to Art and greeted him enthusiastically. Several times I heard them call him, Jaber. The first time I wasn't sure I'd heard them correctly. My Arabic skills are not what they should be. The second time I heard them call him Jaber, I was sure I'd heard it correctly. I started to smile. When it happened a third time, I started laughing. Art turned and asked me what I was laughing about. "They call you Jaber because of what you did for the Jaber family, right?" I asked.

"Yes," he said, as that contagious smile of his emerged. "I was looking for an Arabic name, and it kind of found me after that event." Art had been given this family's name not as a simple courtesy. He truly became part of the family. The Jaber family are Palestinian farmers in the Beqa'a Valley near Hebron. Their land, bit by bit, was being confiscated by the Israeli military and Israeli settlers. A nearby settlement was consistently expanding onto the Jaber family farm. Frequently, these expansions were supported by Israeli soldiers. Other times, it was settler violence that prevented the Jaber family from being able to do anything to protect their land.

As he had done in the past, Art chose to stand in the way. The Jaber family's interactions with the settlers dated back to 1975 when their eldest son had his legs crushed due to the negligence of a settler he was working for. No apology or compensation was ever offered. As time went on, the frequency of their interactions with the settlers and the Israeli military increased. The military confiscated three acres of their land for a road to the Kiryat Arba settlement in 1986. Settlers, in an attempt to scare the Jabers into leaving, sprayed herbicide over their grape crop, killing 400 mature vines in 1989. To build another road for the settlers, the Israeli military confiscated more farmland, destroying $1400 worth of crops in 1995. In 1999, six acres of their orchard was bulldozed by the military (Gish). The Jaber family has land deeds for their land that date back to the Ottoman Empire.

Art decided to make regular visits to the Jaber family home in 2000 when the settler harassment intensified. They destroyed $500 worth of irrigation pipes in the Jaber's fields and later went on a rampage, attacking the family's home. They smashed windows, destroyed the garden, and threw stones. This became an all-too-frequent occurrence. It terrified the family. One of the positive effects of Art's presence in the home, was that the Israeli military was more likely to restrain the settlers when an international or Israeli peace activist was present. The Jabers, a Muslim family, have frequently hosted Christian and Jewish peace activists in their home.

This is a home that already had 11 family members, representing three generations, crammed into it. They had another house built nearby, but the settlers had taken it. On a day that Art wasn't visiting the Jabers, 40 settlers attacked homes in the area and shot 13-year-old Monsur Jaber in the stomach and hand. Ultimately, in the midst of this chaotic environment, Art decided to live with the Jaber family full time.

This is why many of the settlers hated this gentle man. He quietly, peacefully, and consistently stood in their way. He stood with the weak against the strong. The last time I saw Art, he was working in a small village helping to defend the people there from settler attacks. His bed was a slab of stone outside. It was January. Israel's average temperature at night in January is 39 degrees, and it rains frequently.

Art is an excellent example of the CPT philosophy of *getting in the way*. Often nonviolence is confused with pacifism. Most activists will distinguish the two by describing pacifism as a passive act: the choice to not do something such as go to war. Nonviolence, on the other hand, is an active and perhaps even aggressive choice to take action. The philosophy of CPT arose from a call in 1984 for Christians to devote the same discipline and self-sacrifice to nonviolent peacemaking that armies devote to war. They are willing to fight and die for a cause, but not to kill.

I wish I could say the story of the Jaber family had a happy ending, but this is not a made-for-TV movie, and Art doesn't wear a cape. Happy endings are hard to find in this land. The Jabers still courageously hold onto what's left of their land against tremendous odds (Gish). Abdel Jawad, the family's 71-year-old patriarch, walks with a crutch these days. Two years ago, Harsina settlers, on top of a huge wall built on the Jaber's land right behind their house, began throwing stones down on Jaber grandchildren playing in their backyard. While attempting to save the toddlers, Abdel tripped on the stony ground and broke his pelvis (Christian Peacemaker Teams "News Archive").

On March 28, 2008, 40 armed Israeli settlers guarded by three jeeploads of Israeli soldiers destroyed a Jaber grape arbor at the corner of the settlers-only entrance road to Harsina Settlement and Highway 60. They sawed down 23 grape vines. Some of the vines were as old as 30 years and about three inches across at the base (Christian Peacemaker Teams "News Archive"). The Jabers still hold on.

STANDING IN THE WAY

The words gentle and powerful rarely go together in our culture. That's an unfortunate limitation. It is truly a beautiful synergy to witness. Art doesn't seem to accept modern conventional definitions of power. Force and power are not synonymous to him. On a day when he was walking children to school in Hebron, he encountered Israeli soldiers who said the children were not allowed to go to school today. Feeling fairly sure the soldiers would not shoot him and absolutely convinced that the children had a right to attend school, Art looked at the children and said, "Let's just go." Art describes how the automatic rifles, the very symbol of modern power, hung uselessly at the soldiers sides.

This is the beauty of the nonviolent approach. If you are willing to die to defend the rights of others, your action forces the moral choice on those who are trying to deny those rights. They have to wrestle with the ideology they serve. Is it worth killing for? This old man is willing to peacefully die for his cause. Are you willing to kill for yours?

The slogan, *getting in the way*, means more than physically standing between those with the guns and their intended victims. It's also a reference to the member's Christian faith. Their goal is to get in the way or to use the path of Christ, to follow his example. Art exemplifies this in ways I've rarely witnessed before. Growing up in a Christian family and community, faith was discussed frequently and in depth. As an adult, I have spent most of my life living in Christian communities with many good people. Yet, self-sacrifice and unconditional love, two hallmarks of Christ's life, are rarely displayed even among good people.

Art always greets Israeli settlers and soldiers with, "Shalom," a greeting meaning, peace, as he walks around Hebron. I observed this once when a group of Israeli soldiers marched through the central Hebron market place with automatic weapons leveled. Palestinian shop owners quickly moved back into their shops. Art stepped directly into their path and said, "Shalom. Shalom." They looked at him and his CPT hat with clear expressions of disgust on their faces. They would not return his greeting of peace.

The Israeli settlers, on the other hand, often reply by attacking him either verbally or physically. In 1997, when a settler approached Art and struck him while he was walking down the street, Art's reply was, "Shabat Shalom." It was the Sabbath so the traditional greeting is modified to reflect that (Hebron Journal 92). This is essentially the equivalent of saying, "Peace be with you" and "Have a nice day," right after someone struck you.

Yet the phrase is really deeper than that. It is a phrase used to wish the peace of the Sabbath to each other. Further, it is used to reference God as the "common Creator and Father, and that His intention for humankind was our peace and happiness" (Shabbat Shalom). Art is not simply refraining from responding to violence with violence. He is also holding these settlers accountable to their own moral code by his words and his deeds.

This is turning the other cheek in the truest sense of that phrase. I do not say this simply because he didn't strike back. There is more to Christ's admonition to turn the other cheek than resisting the urge to strike back. Interpretation of the Sermon on the Mount passage must be read in the context of its historical moment. In Jewish society at the time of Christ, striking someone you viewed as lower class with the back of the right hand was used to assert dominance and authority. If that person *turned the other cheek*, you would be faced with a dilemma. They are turning their face toward the backhand blow and thus, not giving you a cheek to backhand. The left hand at that time was used only for unclean purposes, so a backhand strike on the opposite cheek was not possible. The only alternative would be to slap the person with an open hand, which would be viewed as a challenge. This was something only done to equals in that society. Thus, by turning the other cheek, the person is refusing to be humiliated and demanding equality (Wink). It is from this example of active nonviolence given by Christ, that many people in the nonviolent movement draw their inspiration.

❧ THE MARCH ❧

Art is just one example of many remarkable people who work for CPT. During a curfew imposed by the Israeli military, a peaceful march to worship at the Ibrahimi Mosque was planned by the Palestinian residents of Hebron. They wanted to demonstrate for the rights of free assembly and freedom to worship. During curfews in Hebron, the Palestinian residents are barred from leaving their homes, yet the Israeli settlers are free to move and worship where they like. If a Palestinian leaves their home, it can lead to arrest or the distinct possibility of being shot by the soldiers.

CPT decided to participate in the march to prevent a violent confrontation with the soldiers or settlers. They invited Palestinian journalists who worked for major news agencies such as Reuters, to cover the march. Many of these journalists had been beaten by Israeli soldiers before, but were willing to risk it again to cover this march. Several members of CPT, in their bright red hats and arm bands, walked in front of the march to make it clear to the soldiers that this was a peaceful march.

As the marchers neared the curfew zone, a squad of Israeli soldiers in full riot gear came charging down the alley straight at the marchers. Two members of CPT and a Palestinian leader leapt in front of the soldiers with their hands in the air yelling, "Don't shoot! This is nonviolent! They're not throwing stones." The soldiers were in firing positions and the CPT members had their bodies directly in the way of the guns, which are pointed at the front of a crowd containing many children. More CPT members moved to the front.

The soldiers fired percussion grenades into the crowd. The effects of these can vary from simply causing one to go deaf for a while to severe burns and bruising. A Palestinian child in the front of the crowd was an unfortunate victim of all three. The explosion and the flame from these grenades in an already-chaotic situation can be terrifying. The Palestinian leadership turned to the young men in the march and yelled, "No stones! No stones!"

While the march was based upon the principles of nonviolence, it's impossible to completely prevent small numbers of uninvited people from joining a large march. This presents a problem for the Palestinian leaders of the march. It's pretty much guaranteed that the marchers will be provoked or abused at some point by soldiers. When this happens, it is absolutely crucial that the leaders keep the crowd calm and focused on the principles of nonviolence. If young Palestinian men have joined the march, and if their threshold for abuse by the soldiers is not as high, the leadership may not be able to control them when the abuse comes. Thus begins a downward spiral. Once the stones fly, the soldiers feel free to fire on the crowd, and everything that the march represents will evaporate amidst the blood, screams, and gunfire.

Stones were not thrown, and the standoff was broken by an angry soldier plowing through the crowd with his shield and body armor knocking people aside. An enraged cry erupted from the young Palestinian men in the back of the crowd. Again, the leaders yelled, "No stones!" Some of the soldiers took up firing positions. The CPT members again jump in front of the guns. The soldiers are physically stopped by one of their officers grabbing hold of them.

It's crucial to control the young men on both sides of a standoff like this. This is where the greatest possibility for violence resides. Fortunately, there were leaders on both sides trying to avoid bloodshed. Unfortunately, this was not true of all of them. An Israeli police commander pushed his way to the front of the line and began to scream at a CPT member named Pierre Shantz. The man was inches from Pierre as he screamed and spit flew from his mouth. Without anger, Pierre explained that this was a nonviolent march and the commander needed to keep his soldiers under control.

The commander struck Pierre in the face three times. Pierre's only response was, that this incident would be recorded in his CPT report. The commander responded by having Pierre arrested by the Israeli civilian police. Sara Reschley, another CPT member who had stood in front of the guns, asked why Pierre was being arrested. The commander had her arrested, too.

The standoff continued as the tension between the two sides mounted. The march leaders realized that all it would take was one angry young man with a stone to give the soldiers the excuse to fire on the crowd. And then something remarkable happened. The Palestinian leadership announced it was time to pray. When the announcement was made, immediately an Israeli officer, who was of the Druze faith and spoke Arabic, realized what the leaders were trying to do. He walked into the crowd of Palestinian young men and began to help the leadership by encouraging the young men to pray. Though the young men must have viewed the act as somewhat humorous and completely surreal, they complied. How often had they experienced an Israeli officer encouraging them to pray (Gish Personal interview)?

The crowd dropped to the ground in prayer. This was one of those odd scenes that I've seen at protests since then, yet it never ceases to move me. Even a cursory Internet search for photos from the Bil'in weekly protests will provide the reader with images like this: a large crowd of Palestinians on the ground apparently bowing toward a group of Israeli soldiers. The soldiers have facial expressions that range from indifference to disgust. The disconnect between what the image appears to convey and what it actually means is striking.

At first glance, the image conveys a group of people who seem to be bowing to a group with a superior force of arms, a conquered people giving up. In reality, here is a group of people who are not conquered, but triumphant in the face of an overwhelming military force. They are exercising freedom of religion in the very face of a force that has the power of life and death. Ignoring the guns pointed directly at them, they submit themselves to a higher power with seeming indifference to their own mortality.

At the conclusion of the prayers, the march leaders declared the march over and returned home. CPT left with them, leaving any angry young men who should decide to throw stones to face the consequences of their actions alone. This is the type of work that CPT does in Hebron day in and day out. I am loath to imagine how the march would have ended had CPT not been there that day.

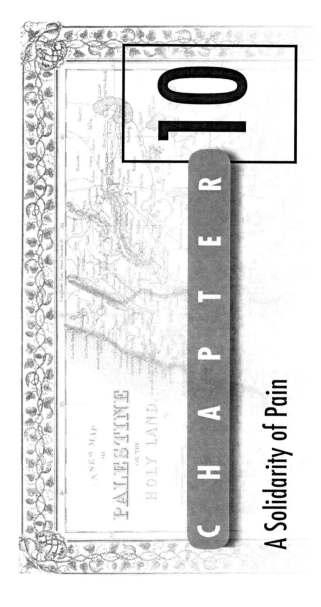

CHAPTER 10

A Solidarity of Pain

✄ THE RÉSUMÉ ✄

"I am the son of a holocaust survivor: My father is an Auschwitz graduate …

Sixty years ago when my forefathers were sent to the crematoriums in Europe, the free and civilized world stood aloof and did not lift a finger to save them. Today, too, 60 years later while these two mad nations are mercilessly butchering one another, the world again looks the other way and does nothing to put a stop to the killing and this is a shame! And this is a crime!!! All I have left is to beseech you not to behave that way. Do not stand aloof. Be involved and concerned because we are talking about your future and ours. Not everyone must think the same. It is possible and necessary to argue, but to turn your backs on reality, to stick your heads in the sand and to live in a bubble is wrong, because you know: bubbles tend to burst in your face sometimes…

And I thank you all, from the bottom of my heart, for listening. For me that is the most important thing of them all. To have the ability to listen and the ability to talk to each other. We must be prepared to listen to 'the other.' Because if we don't listen to the other's story, we won't be able to understand the source of his pain and we should not expect the other to understand our own pain.

Here is where it begins and here it will end" (Elchanan). ***Grammar modified)

This is a remarkable statement, but the context in which it was uttered takes it to a whole different level. Rami Elchanan made this statement years after, as he would put it, his bubble burst. The bubble exploded on the first day of school. His 14-year-old daughter went to shop for school books on Ben Yehuda Street. As she and her friends walked down the street, I imagine them giggling and chatting at light speed, the way that only 14-year-old girls can do. What I cannot imagine — what I do not allow myself to imagine — is what the carnage would look like after two suicide bombers exploded themselves in the middle of the crowded street. Five people were killed, including these three little girls on their first day of school.

Rami describes that day:

It was a Thursday at three in the afternoon — and the beginning of a long night, cold and dark…

At first in the depths of your heart, you hope that the terrible finger won't point at you this time. You find yourself running crazily through the streets, going from one police station to the next, one hospital to the next, until eventually, much later in that long, accursed night, you find yourself in the morgue and this terrible finger is right between your eyes and you see a sight that you will never, ever, be able to blot out.

I didn't know how to approach a man with a résumé of pain such as this. Obviously, this was a dilemma with many of the people I interviewed for this book. What right do I have to ask anything of someone who's been through something such as this? My résumé appears piti-fully anemic in their presence. I can almost hear the flap of the vulture's wings as I write the questions for the interview. It's difficult not to view this as preying upon someone else's tragedy, regardless of my good intentions. In addition to this, due to my own personal circumstances, the death of a daughter his particularly hard. It's not right, but it is reality.

❈ A SCHIZOPHRENIC EXISTENCE ❈

I've walked Ben Yehuda Street many times. It's a very glitzy and glamorous street. High-end shops line both sides of the street as you walk down it. Shoppers are everywhere. It seems so removed from the violence of this conflict. People sip cups of expensive coffee, chat, and play on their laptops. In some ways, you could be in Paris or New York, but you're not. You are in Jerusalem.

This is the rather schizophrenic life lived by many Israelis. In many ways, living in Jerusalem or Tel Aviv is a very pleasant existence filled with modern conveniences. One is surrounded by wealth and beauty, until a bomb rips through this pleasant reality. Then the other reality, the darker reality, lands with both feet.

I think many, if not most, Israelis could identify with Rami's description of how he hoped the terrible finger of fate would not point at him this time. As he said those words, I thought back to an afternoon I spent in Tel Aviv. I was writing in a beach side café, killing time until my flight home. I had just spent some time in the West Bank, and the opulence that surrounded me in this area of Tel Aviv was a shock to the system.

I watched as people enjoyed the sun and sand. I couldn't help but think of the irony that just a few miles away, a much shorter distance than I drive to work every day, was a very different reality in the West Bank. Just as I was thinking about this, I heard a familiar sound. Yet it was not a sound I'd heard in Tel Aviv before. The deep, pulsating sound of the rotors got louder. I looked up and saw several Israeli gunships fly right along the beach. Surely, this would shatter the idyllic illusion of this beach scene. It didn't. No one looked up. No one stopped what they were doing. No one even flinched. The grandfather and his grandson playing paddle ball didn't miss a beat. What young boy wouldn't look up to see a gunship fly by? My guess is this: one who had seen it too many times.

It is truly amazing and tragic what humans can get used to. I thought of an old Palestinian woman I had observed shopping for fruit many years ago in the West Bank. She was simply shopping for fruit on the streets of Ramallah, as I'm sure she did most every day. But this, to me, was not a normal day. Clouds of tear gas rolled down the street. Rocks were thrown. Israeli soldiers were firing their weapons. Military snipers emerged from their rooftop positions. My vision was distorted in my lungs, burned from the tear gas. As I looked across the street, the old woman thumped the melons for ripeness. I yelled in Arabic "Ma'am, get out of the street. They're shooting." A more obvious statement could not have been uttered if I'd sat up all night planning it. She gave no visible sign that she heard me. As I yelled again, I saw soldiers emerging from the tear gas coming toward us, and I knew it was too late. So I ran across the street in a desperate attempt to push her out of the firing line. It turned out to be a rather comical attempt at heroics, for just as I crossed the street, she calmly walked from the fruit stand to an alleyway door that was 10 yards away. She was out of harm's way. At one level, she was probably never in it. Her timing was every bit as impeccable as mine was lousy. As I reached the fruit stand, she closed the door and the cloud of tear gas rolled over me. The soldiers were not far behind. I ran down the alleyway, bouncing like a pinball off the walls, unable to see and barely able to breathe. I was wrong about many things that day, but this was chief among them: it *was* just a normal day, for her.

For the Palestinians, the darker reality of the conflict is ever-present. The military occupation surrounds them in the form of soldiers, walls, checkpoints, and poverty. Death is a constant companion. They die in this conflict at a much higher rate than the Israelis. Sometimes, their death toll is five times higher. Sometimes, it's 10 times higher. In the Gaza War it was over one hundred times higher. One would think that the significant differences between the Palestinian world and the Israeli world would make it difficult for them to communicate with one another. Beyond these differences lie the obvious reasons to hate one another. One would think this would make dialogue across this bloody gulf impossible. One would be wrong.

Rami is part of an organization known as the Parents Circle – Families Forum. This organization is, as far as I know, without precedent. Palestinians and Israelis who have lost family members to violence in the conflict, meet together as a force for reconciliation and peace. People who have experienced some of the greatest losses in the conflict come together in a solidarity of pain.

Rami described to me what it was like to attend his first meeting. Remarkable Israeli peace activists like Yaakov Guterman and Roni Hirshenson arrived. These are people who had every reason to be filled with hate and bitterness but chose a different path. Yaakov Guterman had survived the Holocaust and moved to Israel only to lose his son in the First Lebanon War. Roni Hirshenson had lost both his sons, one to a suicide bomber and the other to suicide by his own hand, in response to the pain of this conflict. Again, here is a résumé of pain that few of us can imagine. Yet, these men refuse to hate or allow their pain to be used in the name of greater violence.

After Rami observed these remarkable people arrive, something happened that had an even deeper impact. He watched as Palestinian families who had lost loved ones in the conflict descended the stairs of the bus. People who had every reason to hate the part of him that represented an Israeli government that had killed their family members, hugged and cried with him over his loss. They had chosen a different path in response to their résumé as well.

He describes the incident as a lightning bolt that came from nowhere. The force of its blow "cracked his programming." He spoke about how one grows up with Palestinians all around you, and yet you really don't know them. They are the day laborers and taxi drivers, but you never touch the humanity of these people. Years and years of demonization prevent you from seeing them as truly human. This meeting changed all that for Rami (Elchanan).

The Parents Circle – Families Forum goes beyond bringing the two sides of the conflict together. Once together, the two sides form a compelling force for peace. They give speaking tours all over the world as well as in Israeli and Palestinian high schools. Rami stated that he felt speaking to these young adults was crucial because they would soon be soldiers. If he could impact just one of them to think before pulling the trigger, he could prevent one Palestinian or Israeli family from entering the world of pain, in which he resides. Often, the speaking tours are given by one Israeli and one Palestinian. One such team is Khaled and Boaz.

❧ **"WHATEVER HAPPENS, WE MUST NOT LOSE HOPE"** ❧

In some ways, it was an extraordinary day, but in too many others, it was simply another day in the occupation. Yasser Arafat had died, and the funeral would take place on this day. Funerals are dangerous events in a conflict such as this. Emotions run high, and simply seeing something or someone that represents the other side — the side that you believe killed your father, your daughter, or your leader, can ignite the conflict all over again. As a result, Israeli soldiers were ordered to stay out of the city center while the funeral procession took place. But this is the West Bank, and what is supposed to happen, rarely does (Parents Circle).

An Israeli military jeep enters the village center. To the mourners, its very presence mocked the ceremony taking place. Predictably, some stones, the symbol of resistance, were thrown. And the all too common reply came. The soldiers fired live rounds into the crowd. Two students fell to the ground. Jamil would never rise again. He was dead. Muayad was injured badly, and the blood came fast, but he was still alive, for now. Yet, considering the checkpoints between him and the hospital that he needed to go to, how much longer would this be true?

In a completely different world, Khaled and Boaz stood before a group of high school students telling their stories. The stories were a beautiful mixture of pain and hope. This is the common thread that joins all the stories of the Parents Circle members. Hundreds of families, both Palestinian and Israeli, join hands in this ritual of retelling their own personal catastrophes two people at a time. These two people stood in a Jewish kibbutz.

With tremendous courage, Khaled, a Palestinian, stood in front of this group of Israelis. Under any other circumstances, as a Palestinian, he would not be allowed to set foot on this kibbutz. Khaled begins to tell about how his brother Yussef was shot by a soldier in their home village. Yussef was married and the father of two children. A few months after Yussef's death, Khaled's younger brother Sa'ed was shot and killed as well.

Since I was not at this meeting, I am forced to imagine the setting. As Khaled attempts to sift some hope for the future out of the ashes of his past, there is a knock at the door. Boaz steps into the hallway to talk to the messenger. I imagine the terrible finger that Rami described circling over the school like a bird of prey. Khaled tries to ignore the sounds of its wings while bringing a message of hope. I imagine Boaz returning to whisper in Khaled's ear. I imagine the paleness of Khaled's face as the terrible finger lands.

The 15-year-old boy lying on the ground bleeding at Arafat's funeral was Khaled's son. If something wasn't done soon, he, like the other young man, would never rise again. Khaled's last words to the students at the kibbutz as he left were, "Listen to me. Whatever happens, we must not lose hope. We must not stray from the path of reconciliation." Here again, I do not have the words to describe a man like this. They would be insufficient to describe character such as this.

A joint effort by Israeli and Palestinian members of the Parent's Circle manage to get the boy special permission to be taken to a hospital in Jerusalem. When he arrives, his blood pressure is zero. Khaled waits the long hours in the hallway as the surgery goes on. He is consoled by both Israelis and Palestinians who have a similar résumé of pain. Ultimately, the doctor emerges to tell Khaled that his son will live. He adds that if he had arrived a matter of minutes later, this would not be the case. Although the story ends with this glimmer of hope, the glimmer is shadowed by the question: what if the boy's father didn't have Israeli friends?

One could easily write an entire book about the Parent's Circle and all the people with their amazing stories. The same could be said for all the people and organizations that I write about in this book. As a result, I am constantly faced with painful choices about what to leave in and what to leave out. I feel a tremendous amount of guilt over the people and the stories that don't make it in. This would be particularly true if I did not mention Robi Damelin and Ali Abu Awwad.

Robi's son was killed by a Palestinian sniper while performing his compulsory military service. The sniper had no way of knowing that her son was also a member of the peace movement. He simply knew that her son wore an Israeli military uniform. The uniform reminded him of family members and friends who had died at the hands of other Israeli soldiers. He pulled the trigger, and the soldier and the peace activist fell to the ground never to rise again. When the soldier's colleagues recovered the body, they found a book in his pocket. It was the Israeli army code of ethics. The West Bank is a place where irony thrives.

Ali had rejected the violence of the second intifada. But you do not need to be involved to get dragged in. An Israeli settler drove down the road near his village, randomly shooting at Palestinians. One person lay dead on the ground, and Ali was hit in the leg. His last memory of his brother, was of him crying as Ali was taken away to the hospital. His brother had been both his mother and his father, during the years when his mother was imprisoned by the Israelis. Ali described his brother has his *whole world*. That world was shattered by a bullet to the brain. An Israeli soldier shot Ali's brother in the head when he returned to his home village one day.

Robi Damelin and Ali Abu Awwad are not victims of their pain. They use the pain to fuel their passion for finding an end to this conflict. They've given many talks in Israel, the West Bank, and all over the world. Their efforts are showcased in a documentary called, Encounter Point. After her son was killed, Robi wrote a letter to the mother of the Palestinian sniper who had taken his life. In a courageous gesture that illustrates the integrity of her beliefs, she invited the mother and her son to meet with her in an attempt at reconciliation. Again, words are insufficient.

It was a wrong number. Natalia had called her friend in Jerusalem, but the phone rang in Gaza. No one picked up. The story typically would have ended there, but the phone belonged to a man named, Jihad. Jihad is a word that resonates in the Western mind with such dark overtones, that one can almost hear the theme song to *Jaws* playing in the background when the word is uttered. We generally hear the word translated as, holy war, although it has several meanings.

Jihad seems to be a man that more closely resembles one of the other meanings of the word. It also means an internal struggle to purify oneself. Jihad noticed the call on his phone and returned it. Due to the openness of these two individuals, neither one did what many on both sides of this conflict would've done: hang up. The conversation ranged widely. Jihad was amazed to find an Israeli who was so open and understanding. Natalia was amazed to learn how bad things were in Gaza due to Israeli military policy. Jihad explained how food rotted at the checkpoints and that his wife was expecting a baby any day now. He had no way of getting to the hospital. Soon Natalia and Jihad introduced each other to friends and family, and the network grew. Thus, what began as a conversation, has launched over a million more conversations between Israelis and Palestinians funded by the Hello Peace program.

Inspired by the story of this first conversation, the Parent's Circle created the Hello Peace program. The project is a free phone line enabling Israelis and Palestinians to talk to each other. They simply call the free number and specify what type of person they would like to talk to (such as male or female, religious or secular). They are then connected to someone fitting that description on the other side of the conflict. For each conversation, they are given 30 minutes of free time to talk. They are allowed to talk as often as they like.

Remarkable things happen when enemies are allowed to talk past all the checkpoints, the media, and the Wall. To keep an entire group of people as an eternal enemy, it's necessary to strip them of their humanity. They must become monsters. If we don't do this, our natural instincts and our sympathy muddy the simple black-and-white image we have in our minds. Hello Peace facilitates this process.

Israeli families receive calls from the new Palestinian friends after a suicide bombing, just to make sure they are all right. Palestinians ask Israeli callers to speak to their children, so they can learn that not all Israelis are like the soldiers they meet in the streets. One Israeli family regularly meets their Palestinian friends at a checkpoint to give them insulin. The Palestinian family has a diabetic son, and some medicine is difficult to come by in the West Bank.

Even people who directly opposed one another in the past, find a way to discover the other's humanity. Sammy and Arik became friends on the phone line and later discovered through the course of conversation, that Arik had been a soldier that occupied Sammy's home town of Ramallah. Arik told Sammy how he hated serving in the military because he was forced to police a civilian population, which involved "causing harm to innocent people." Sammy remarked that, before the conversation, he "thought Israelis didn't care at all when innocent Palestinians suffer and are killed." He continued, "But now I know they do care, and I have hope that there can be peace" (Parent's Circle).

There are several key elements of the project exemplified in Sammy's statement. First, to have a lasting peace, it is necessary to shatter some of the misconceptions that each side has of the other. Roni Hirshenson, of the Parents Circle, put it this way: "The pain on both sides is identical. Our goal is to increase empathy on both sides. Right now, our images of each other are controlled by the media and our leaders. Israelis see Palestinians as terrorists, and Palestinians see Israelis as soldiers and settlers. This must change." Yaniv, a 22-year-old Israeli who had recently finished his military service, is a good example of this. After talking to Palestinians on Hello Peace, he said,

> *"I heard many, at least 10, say they are against suicide bombers and support peace. It is important for us Israelis to know that there are Palestinians who feel this way. Because when we see all those pictures on TV, we think there are no normal people on the other side and they feel exactly the same way."*

This is the second key aspect of Hello Peace. It demonstrates that there's someone on the other side to talk to. Robi Damelin says it this way: "Obviously, not every conversation is gentle and loving. The only rule is that you listen. Israeli leaders keep saying there is no one to talk to, and we wanted to show that that's not true." Prime Minister Olmert and Defense Minister Netanyahu have made statements to this effect. Last year, Netanyahu stated, "there is simply no Palestinian partner" (Israel Insider).

Rhetoric like this reinforces the misconceptions that people already have about the conflict.

Yet, the stories that come out of Hello Peace in particular and the Parent's Circle, more broadly shine a spotlight on these political clichés from the moral high ground in which they reside. Yitzhak Frankenthal, a man who lost his entire family in the Holocaust and later lost his son in this conflict, makes an assertion that is very hard to ignore. "We, as a group of bereaved parents, who have lost their kids and continue to talk with the Palestinians, we are not looking for revenge, we're not looking for hatred. We're looking to trade reconciliation and peace. *So if we can do it, everyone can and needs to do it*" (Italics added) ("Morning Edition").

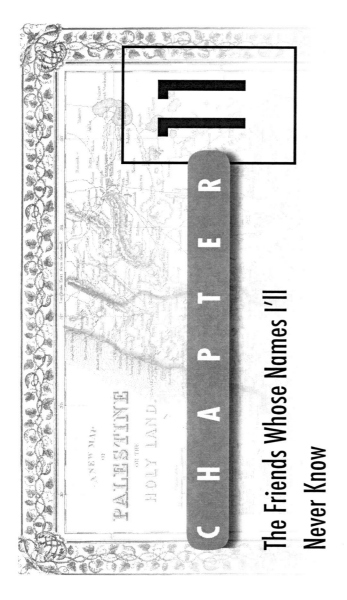

CHAPTER 11

The Friends Whose Names I'll Never Know

※ **EDDIE WAS BLEEDING** ※

Eddie was bleeding. He had been laughing moments before. We were having a great conversation. Conversations with Eddie were always great. Eddie was a hero in every sense of the word. After getting to know Eddie, I have always found popular depictions of heroes with greased and bulging biceps to be rather laughable. Eddie might've been five feet tall, but that would've been generous, and he was thin enough so as to be almost two-dimensional. Now, this hero was bleeding.

To this day, I don't know why he fainted. We were walking out of the café together, holding a conversation, and suddenly I was the only one talking. Perhaps it was low blood sugar, but he had fainted as we exited the café and was now lying in a pool of his own blood. He cracked his skull on the concrete when he fell. I had been living in the West Bank for over a month now and had seen a significant amount of violence, so perhaps this shouldn't have shocked me, but it did.

As is often the case with head wounds, he was bleeding rather quickly. There was not much time to get him the help he needed. A group of people started to gather. I started yelling in rather poor Arabic for someone to call an ambulance, as I knelt next to Eddie trying to slow his bleeding. When the people around me didn't move as fast as I thought they should, I grew angry. From my position on the floor, I grabbed the man nearest me by his shirt and pulled him down to floor level. I asked him why no one was moving as I called for an ambulance. He had a strange expression on his face that I don't believe I'll ever forget. It's the same expression that a parent has when they try to explain something to a child, they know the child cannot comprehend. It is an expression of sadness and frustration rolled into one. As I looked from his face to others in the crowd, it became clear to me that they were all feeling this.

"We have no ambulances here," he said.

"Then get me a taxi. I'll take him to the hospital," I yelled.

"We have no hospitals here," he replied with the same level of sadness.

"Of course, there are. I've seen a hospital in a town just a few miles from here."

"Yes. But we are not allowed to go there without going through the checkpoint and that usually takes written permission from the government."

"How long does that usually take?"

"About nine months."

"So you have to plan your accidents here nine months in advance?"

"Yes. Something like that," he made a pained attempt to smile at my sarcasm.

"I've lived here long enough to see many people bleed. You must have some way of dealing with it without waiting nine months."

"Yes, we do. I've called a man with a car. He will take you to a woman in the village who can help."

This was my first trip to the Middle East. It was during the first uprising between Palestinians and Israelis. I was in my early 20s, and this incident brought home the everyday reality of life under military occupation. Simple everyday accidents, easily remedied where I grew up by a trip to the hospital, could result in death. Over 991 incidents of denial of access to ambulances for Palestinians have been reported. Eighty-three deaths have resulted from the prevention of access to medical services (Palestine Monitor). These numbers, of course, do not include those Palestinians who see no point in reporting it. Many I've spoken to do not. The Palestinians of the West Bank have been living this way for over 40 years.

❧ THE FRIENDS WHOSE NAMES I'LL NEVER KNOW ❧

The woman in the village was able to stitch up Eddie's head. We spent a long sleepless night taking care of him. We were afraid to let him go to sleep for fear of a concussion. Yet, the story does not end here. In fact, this book is a product of the fact that it does not. After living in the West Bank for several months, Eddie went home. When he arrived at Israel's Ben-Gurion Airport, he went through the normal screening process. Security asked him where he'd been while in Israel. When security found out that he had spent some time in the West Bank, the interview turned much more serious.

"How long were you living in the West Bank?"

"Several months," he replied.

"While you were living there, did you ever meet a Palestinian?"

Eddie begins to laugh at the absurdity of the question, believing it to be an attempt at humor. It wasn't. You can understand his confusion. If you were a visitor from France or Spain and you took a trip to United States for several months, and upon leaving the United States, security asked if you'd ever met an American, you would, at the very least, think it a bit odd. Eddie attempted to swallow his laughter and put on a more serious face.

"Yes sir, I did," he said in answer to the odd question.

"What were their names?" The security man asked.

At this point, any trace of laughter in Eddie evaporated. We had all witnessed, in our time in the West Bank, Palestinian families being punished for crimes they had no part in. Collective punishment by the Israeli military was the rule, not the exception. All too many families have had their homes destroyed because their son was accused of tossing a stone at a tank or an armored personnel carrier. Or you could simply be the family whose home was next to another home when it was destroyed and, as a result, yours gets destroyed as well. Or you could simply be in the wrong place at the wrong time while they were chasing someone, and receive the beating that was intended for him. As all these thoughts raced through Eddie's head, he decided to do something I've never seen him do before. He lied.

"I don't really remember the names," he said reluctantly. Eddie didn't believe in lying. Yet, he couldn't live with the idea that any of the kind, generous, and most importantly, innocent people he had spent time with, would be harmed. At this point, Eddie was taken to another room with new security people. The questions began again. The tone of the security questions shifted more closely to the tone of an interrogation. It's funny: the movies always make interrogations look rather exciting. There's no doubt that there can be exciting moments, but the overwhelming majority of the time, it's the same questions again and again, asked by different people.

Question after question, the hours passed. He missed his flight, and still the questions continued. Always the same ones, slightly rephrased, with different people asking them. He had told them everything he could. He was a Quaker, a man of peace. He works for a Quaker school in the West Bank, donating much of his time. He was a talented and skilled man. He could've chosen to work anywhere in the world and made a lot of money, but he chose to work in the middle of a conflict zone and help children. As more hours passed, even the patience of this man of peace, wore a bit thin. He decided to inject some humor in the process. They asked again:

"What were the names of the people you met?"

"Oh, I think I do remember one of their names," he responded.

"Yes. What was it?" they asked impatiently.

"It was... I think... yes, I remember it now. Mohammed. That's it! It was definitely Mohammed... or something like that."

This answer is roughly the equivalent of answering with the name Joe or John in the United States. They didn't find his response humorous. To make this abundantly clear, a beating followed. After this small Quaker man was beaten, they stripped him naked. Then they began a very thorough, full body-cavity search. As indignity followed beatings, the small naked man was left spread eagle facing a stone wall. To explain the next part of the story, I need to take a definitional digression for a moment. For those of you who don't study political violence, such as myself, a Kalashnikov rifle is the name of a Russian-made AK-47 machine gun. In some parts of the world, the term, *Kalashnikov* has come to mean any AK-47 machine gun. In almost any American movie involving a firefight in a foreign land, these are the rifles the bad guys have. They have a large banana (curved) clip and are approximately three feet long. It is important to keep this last part in mind when reading the following conversation.

"Where did you travel during your time in Israel?"

"I've already told you, I spent several months in the West Bank."

"Did you meet any Palestinians while you were there?"

"Yes. I told you that."

"Did you bring any weapons in the country with you to give to terrorists?"

"I'm a Quaker. We believe in peace."

"Did you bring any weapons in the country with you?"

Eddie responded in his thick Scottish accent: "Yes sir. Ya caught me. I have a Kalashnikov up ma ars. Would ya like to check?"[1]

More beatings ensued. But this is the important part of the story. Eddie flew back to Scotland. He gathered up the rest of his things. He said his goodbyes to his family members, and then he returned to the West Bank: the place where he busted his skull and almost died because he couldn't get through a checkpoint in time, the place where security interrogated him, beat him, and gave him a full body-cavity search. He could work anywhere in the world, but he chose to work there. He could do anything he wanted, but he chose to help those kids.

Eddie's heroic choice is what first inspired me to write this book. The West Bank is full of people making heroic choices for peace, most of them far more costly than Eddie's. That is the point of this book, that there is hope amidst the chaos. Eddie's story also gave me the title for this book. When discussing this story with a good friend of mine, I described how Eddie wrote a letter after his interrogation. It was addressed to some of us who were still living in the West Bank. After he described his interrogation ordeal, he warned us not to learn anyone's last name. The idea being, that if we were interrogated when we left, we would not be able to hurt any innocent people by revealing the names.

This proved exceptionally difficult. When you spend a month or two with people, you grow close under normal circumstances. In the cauldron of a conflict zone, relationships are forged fast and deep. In an environment such as this, to not even learn someone's last name seems to be the height of disrespect. Yet the difficulty does not end there. For years after my first trip to the Middle East, I was unable to return due to family obligations. From time to time, I would receive reports about the Israeli military attacking a particular village. To know that you have friends in that village is difficult enough, but to never be able to find out whether those friends lived or died in the attack? To not be able to help in any way because you never learned their last name? That is a special kind of pain.

---

[1] The overwhelming majority of the quotations in this book are from experiences or interviews conducted in the last few years. Since I was aware that these experiences and interviews could be a part of this book, I consciously took notes to make sure my quotations were as accurate as possible. The story about Eddie happened almost 17 years ago. This is long before I ever dreamed of writing a book. As a result, the quotations in the story about Eddie are not exact. They are my recollections of the conversations that took place many years later.

And so these are the "friends whose names I'll never know."

As I write these words, I look at a picture of myself in a refugee camp on my wall. It's from my first trip over there about 17 years ago. I look at the faces of the young boys gathered round me in the middle of this dusty street. Old dilapidated shacks frame the background of the picture: their homes. The kids ranged in age from about five to 10 years old. My oldest daughter is the age of some of them. Given that this picture was taken 15 years ago, if these children grew up, they would now be approximately 20 to 25 years of age. The key word in that last phrase is *if*. Given what has gone on in the last 15 years, as I look at each of the faces, I must resign myself to the strong possibility that they are today, either dead or in jail.

✂ TELL YOUR PEOPLE WHAT YOU SAW HERE ✂

I guess I've always been amazed by the people in the middle of this conflict. Earlier in this book, I describe a confrontation between myself and several Israeli soldiers. I wanted to avoid leaving two Palestinian students behind at a checkpoint, where their future would be far from certain. After the situation had been resolved and we were on our way to Haifa, a Palestinian woman on the bus approached me and said:

"Thank you for doing what few are willing to do," she began. "We need more people like you here. Will you be staying in Palestine much longer?"

"No, I'll be going home soon. I have promises, made to people back home, that I must keep. But I will definitely return."

The words tasted cowardly as they came out of my mouth. I did indeed have promises to keep back home that were important. Beyond this, the meager sum of money that I had scraped together to be able to come to the Middle East was now gone. I had lost 40 pounds in less than two months, living on about one dollar's worth of food per day, for quite a while. All of these facts seemed irrelevant at the moment. All my cultural influences growing up, from my parents' faith to the movies I had watched, screamed that standing up for the powerless is what you do. I was waiting for the movie's musical score to play and immediately remove all the obstacles that stood in my path to staying in this place and helping these people. But the music never played, and the obstacles stood fast.

She seemed to understand. Many of the Palestinian students around me had noticed my rapid weight loss and commented on it. I had been invited into many homes for dinner, partially due to the Palestinian tradition of hospitality, but also because some of them were clearly worried about me. Indeed, had I chosen to, I could survive there awhile longer simply on the hospitality of strangers. Yet, the same cultural tradition that demanded that I help the powerless also prohibited me from accepting too much charity from them. While my internal struggle went on, she continued.

"I do not doubt that you will return. Anyone could see that in your eyes. But until that time, may I ask one favor of you?"

"Sure, name it."

"When you return home, tell your people what you saw here. Your people are good people. I don't think they know what the Israelis do to us. I don't think they know what their money buys. You've seen a lot while you were here. Just tell them. Promise me that."

"You have my word. I promise." The emotion welling up in my throat wouldn't allow me to say much more than that. This was the first time I was asked this favor, but it was far from the last. I was struck by this. People in the midst of a conflict, with almost nothing in terms of material possessions or rights, and their first instinct was to ask me to tell their story. They didn't ask for money. They didn't ask for guns. They didn't ask for me to help get them out of the country. They simply wanted their story told. This happened to me many times.

✌ THE HEROES YOU NEVER HEAR ABOUT ✌

In the 17 years since that time, I've kept my word. I've been back far more than once. I've spoken to thousands of people about what goes on in the midst of this conflict. Some of them wanted to hear about it. Many of them didn't. I have surprised and often angered family and friends by telling the *other story*, the one that does not fit the narrative we consume here. I have given many public lectures on the topic, at times with people waiting to physically confront me afterwards. I've found that when you explain what really happens on the ground over there, you manage to anger both sides (pro-Israeli and pro-Palestinian) of the debate. Every semester, I use this topic to challenge my students. Yet none of this has ever felt like it was remotely enough.

The guilt I felt for not staying longer that first time has never completely left me. Yet, part of me never left and never moved past that moment. That part of me didn't get on the plane to return to the Land of the Free. It seemed a quintessentially American thing to do, to stay and struggle in a lost cause where people seek only their own freedom. Every time I return to the West Bank, I am reunited with that part of me, and it introduces me to the Palestinians, Israelis, and internationals who struggle in this cause every day.

The pages of this book have introduced you to a few of these people. There are so many more. But hopefully this book is more than simply me telling stories about the tragic conditions on the ground and the peacemakers who fight to change them. I hope it demonstrates that there is some reason for cautious optimism.

I've been called cynical quite often. Perhaps I am. Perhaps I've seen too much. Yet, each time I think I have seen too much, I find another set of eyes, eyes of people who have seen enough tragedy for several lifetimes. Then I realize indeed, how little I've really seen. My point is this: if a cynic can look beyond the blood and bodies and see a kernel of hope, that says something.

Many of the most significant movements to advance human rights in the past were started by small groups of people who were willing to sacrifice sweat, blood, tears, and all too often, their lives. I see these people on the streets of Ramallah, Jerusalem, Bethlehem, and Bil'in.

People like Sami and Abdullah, who walk into the fire every week. They take their beatings without responding in anger or even raising a hand in defense. Sometimes they are joined by thousands, and sometimes by a few dozen. Nevertheless, they push the struggle on with an eye toward not just convincing an enemy but also redeeming a brother.

The Israeli soldiers and settlers who confront them are not their opponents, so much as potential converts to the cause of peace. Indeed, most of the time when these men walk into the fire, they are joined by Israeli peace activists whom they view as brethren in the struggle. Some are former soldiers, such as the members of Combatants for Peace or the Refuseniks. Some are Israelis like Neta Golan who have devoted their lives to this cause.

This is a remarkable image – every bit as remarkable as white Americans joining hands with black Americans on the streets of America, during the civil rights movement. In fact, it's more remarkable to me due to the fact that some members of both ethnic communities, who have access to automatic weapons, view these peacemakers as traitors. These peacemakers are under threat by their own people as well as those on the other side of the conflict. Yes, this image is amazing, but is this the image you see in your TV screen?

✖ BEING ON THE RIGHT SIDE OF HISTORY ✖

Perhaps the cynic has become the romantic now. We are told again and again that this is clearly a battle of ancient hatreds that will only end with the annihilation of one side or the other. Yet, this conflict has *not* been going on forever. It is a product of the twentieth century, and like so many other conditions that seemed as if they would last forever, it will end. When I was a kid, people used adjectives with the same eternal and epic qualities to describe the troubles in Ireland. In fact, right before my first trip to the Middle East, a massive truck bomb ripped through downtown London, destroying a medieval church and the Liverpool Street underground station, causing hundreds of millions of dollars in damages because the British government decided to erect the famous "ring of steel" around the city.

Today, violence between the two sides in this conflict is much more rare. In 2005, the IRA announced a new era where it would unequivocally renounce violence. They instructed IRA members "to assist the development of purely political and democratic programs through exclusively political means." Further, they announced that "all IRA units have been ordered to dump arms" and "to complete the process to verifiably put its arms beyond use" ("Irish Republican Army").

In 2006, a report by the Independent Monitoring Commission in Northern Ireland indicated that the IRA had ceased all paramilitary activity. The commission declared that "the IRA's campaign is over." Shortly after this, local government was restored to Northern Ireland. Power was shared between these old enemies. Rev. Ian Paisley, leader of the Democratic Unionists, and Martin McGuinness, of Sinn Fein, were sworn in as leader and deputy leader, respectively, of the Northern Ireland executive government. Paisley said, "I believe we are starting on a road to bring us back to peace and prosperity." British prime minister, Tony Blair said, "Look back, and we see centuries marked by conflict, hardship, even hatred among the people of these islands." He said, "Look forward, and we see the chance to shake off those heavy chains of history" ("Irish Republican Army").

This is a conflict that has existed as an open, bleeding sore on the world stage, far longer than the Palestinian-Israeli conflict. It has been going on for centuries. It has been discussed publicly many times, with the same intonations of hopelessness that the Palestinian-Israeli conflict is often shrouded in today. Yet, today there is clear evidence of significant and historic progress. People no longer describe this conflict as one that has been going on forever and will always be. They used to. These enemies found the ability to "shake off those heavy chains of history."

We see this again and again throughout history. There are certain conflicts or even undemocratic institutions, that we proclaim as eternal. Yet, the one common theme among all of these, is that they eventually all come to an end. Even the quintessential conflict that's used as a metaphor for unending conflict, the Hatfields and the McCoys, ended in 1891. In fact, in 1979 the descendents of the two families appeared on the game show, "Family Feud" illustrating that the feud had become something of a punch line.

Beyond conflicts that are mistakenly described as eternal, we often do this with institutions. I've already described how people as bright as Thomas Jefferson made this mistake with slavery, but there are other examples. Many people felt that women would never attain the right to vote. Yet, this right was ultimately achieved through tactics not unlike those used by the people I describe in this book. When Alice Paul led a peaceful protest march for the National American Women's Suffrage Association, she and many other women in the march were physically attacked by men who were offended by the very notion of women's suffrage. While the attack took place, the police stood by and watched (Alice Paul Institute).

Significant social change has frequently started with a small group of very committed people, who stand in the path of the mainstream culture and remind us that things don't have to be this way: They can be better. We as a people, can be better.

February 1, 1960, four black college students sat down at the whites-only lunch counter at the Woolworth's store in Greensboro, North Carolina, and tried to order something to eat. They were looking for more than drinks and doughnuts. They were challenging the very foundation of the social order of the time. The unspoken rules of society required black people to stay out of certain areas of white-owned restaurants, to sit in the rear of city buses, and to use only designated drinking fountains and restrooms (Rutledge).

The nonviolent stand that these students took against the racist institutions of the time, resulted in them being insulted, threatened, and assaulted. It also spawned similar protests and resulted in the desegregation of the Woolworth's lunch counter. Within a week of the their first sit-in protest, their numbers grew from four to one thousand. Yet, as is frequently the case, it was a small, committed core group that made the difference. Here's a comment from one of the original four at the lunch counter, that illustrates the point:

"What people won't talk (about), what people don't like to remember, is that the success of that movement in Greensboro is probably attributed to no more than eight or 10 people," McCain says. "I can say this: when the television cameras stopped rolling and we didn't have eight or 10 reporters left, the folks left. I mean, there were just a very faithful few. McNeil and I can't count the nights and evenings that we literally cried because we couldn't get people to help us staff a picket line."

Small committed groups are having impacts all over the world these days in many different types of settings. Pro-democracy groups have dramatically changed the political landscape in recent years. The largest Muslim country in the world traded in a dictator for a constitution in the late 1990s. Indonesia was revolutionized by this nonviolent, pro-democracy movement. The list of countries that have toppled dictatorships through nonviolent movements recently, includes such diverse countries as Chile, Bolivia, Mali, Nepal, Madagascar, Czechoslovakia, Serbia, Ukraine, Philippines, and Indonesia.

Can things change in the Middle East? Yes, if the peacemakers involved are willing to work and sacrifice everything for it. I hope this book demonstrates that there are many people out there willing to do this. Things can change. The real question is: Which side of history do we want to be on?

POSTSCRIPT

You could hear the pain and anguish in his voice. As I looked around the room full of people I'd brought to the West Bank, there was not a dry eye in the house. I've heard and seen a lot in conflict zones over the years and one could make the case that I've hardened a bit, but as this man spoke of the decisions he was forced to make, tears fell onto the floor in front of me, before I even felt them on my cheeks. I was so lost in his horrible world, I forgot to check my emotions as I usually do.

The man had seven children. As he spoke I heard the sound of carnage behind him. Occasionally he would break off from speaking to me and my group to yell orders to those around him whom he was trying to protect. It was January of 2009 and this was the Gaza War.

He lived in the very heart of darkness at this time. The apartment where he and his children lived saw bombings by Israeli aircraft continuously. There was no way out. Each day he would risk his life and venture out of his building in search of food for his children. He said again and again, "I have money for food, but there is no food. I have money for medicine, but there is no medicine." He shielded his eyes as he walked the streets. Fragments of the bombing victim's bodies littered the ground. All too often they were his neighbors. All too often they were children. This man had been a relief worker in wars around the world. He'd seen war before but not like this.

I have never written a postscript. I'm not even sure I fully understood the purpose of many of the postscripts I've read. I did not intend to write one for this book. Yet after I completed the rough draft of this book in 2008, I found myself planning another trip into the conflict zone for January of 2009. As the trip approached, the Gaza War broke out. Day after day as images of this horrible conflict appeared on our TV screens, people came to me with a calm and peaceful look on their faces and said things like, "Well, I guess this means you'll be cancelling your trip," or "Gosh, this must be weird for you since you go over there every year," or "Well, maybe things will calm down by next year." These well-intentioned statements generally came from very nice people who didn't know me very well. Those who knew me better had a very different approach to the news stories. Phrases like, "Dear God, you're still gonna go, aren't you?" usually accompanied by a shaking head, were typical. I rarely bothered to explain my reasons for going, because I found it difficult to communicate the idea that it felt like a betrayal to not go. To walk away from friends during a time of crisis seemed to be a wrong so deep you could feel it in your bones. It was not something I could walk away from and live with.

I spoke to the group that I was set to lead to the Mideast and told them that I would understand if they didn't want to go. I would perfectly understand. Everyone one of them said they still wanted to go with me. I received this news with a strange mixture of admiration and anxiety. I was extremely proud of them but I was concerned about my ability to protect them during a ramped-up wartime environment. Conflict zones inherently have dangerous elements to them, but when full-scale war comes, even the small amount of things you can usually count on, go out the window.

This is the group of people that were with me as we listened to the father of seven in Gaza while the violence consumed him. He spoke of his children as their world fell apart. In this environment of constant terror, his 15-year-old daughter had lost the ability to control her bladder. This happens a lot to children in a war zone. One of his other children had become paralyzed from the waist down yet there was not a scratch on her. The war had shattered her emotionally. She could not move. She could not run. The terror had completed its wretched course.

Yet, it was his next decision that leveled me. The bombing in Gaza was continuous. The Israeli military had dropped pamphlets stating they would be bombing his area, therefore civilians should seek shelter. Yet in a cruel turn of events, in previous bombings the Israelis had bombed the typical shelters one would run to for safety like UN facilities, schools, churches, and mosques. The people that hid in these shelters had been warned, too. So where do you send your seven children? His solution was heart breaking. He'd decided to send his seven children to seven different places in the desperate hope that some members of the family would survive. I couldn't help but think that while he was technically right, the decision virtually guaranteed that some of his children would die. I couldn't speak. I couldn't do a thing to help him. The tragic story would find its inevitable conclusion regardless of what I thought or did. Many times before, I had changed situations people said were unchangeable by sheer force of will. I had probably taken too much pride in that fact. But now I watched a man in the jaws of a thing against which my will and pride were, at best, merely spectators.

It was at this point that a Palestinian friend of mine, who is much wiser than myself, said, "Can we pray for you?" The man's response began like this, "Pray for the children. The children here suffer unspeakable horrors. Children should never have this happen to them." He stopped and choked back the emotion that was welling up in his throat. He then said something that knocked the breath completely out of me. He stopped himself and said, "No, No, that's not right. Pray for their children, too. No one's children should have to suffer this." I couldn't speak, I still can't after I tell this story to friends. I have to sit still for a minute until the wave of emotion passes and hope they think it's simply a dramatic pause for effect.

In a war, one expects rage and demonization. It is the very currency in which war trades. I know rage was rising up in my throat as I listened. I know better than this, but as he talked about his daughters, I couldn't help but think of mine. As he expressed a sacrificial love toward his enemies, I could think of nothing but the vengeful demon that would posses my body, if I thought my daughters were about to become a statistic. As I said before, I couldn't speak. I simply nodded to my friend who gracefully finished the call by praying for his friend.

This man asked us to pray for the children of his enemies in a war where his people were dying at more than a 100 to one ratio: over 1,400 Palestinians were killed by the Israeli military. In this war, 12 Israelis were killed by Palestinian militants. From the center of hell, he prays for the children of his enemies. He's a far better man than me. If you're honest, he's probably a better person than you. One thing he's not, is alone. I found others in the midst of this hell praying for their enemies. They were Palestinian Muslims, Palestinian Christians, and Jewish Israelis. This is why I wrote the postscript. As I've said before, there are heroes on both sides.

A few days later I took my group to a worship service at a Jewish synagogue. The rabbi discussed recent events in the war and asked the people to break into small groups to pray. As the groups gathered, he explained that we were not praying for one side to win or the other side to lose. We were praying for those immersed in this conflict regardless of what side they were on.

As the group I was in started to pray, emotions ran high and it was clear a few people did not agree with the rabbi, but most did. That's the point. Most people in this conflict want peace. That's not what we hear on the news here in America. Pundits are paid to divide, not unite. Yet this is indeed the reality.

The following day, I took my group to the worship service of a Palestinian church. The pastor stood in front of a wounded congregation. These people watched the TV screens as their family and friends died in bombing after bombing in Gaza. They were sad and they were angry. With his people dying at a rate of 117 to one, it took remarkable courage for this pastor to stand in front of his congregation, and use words containing anything other than hate and vengeance. That's what many people want to hear in this situation. It's natural. It's an easy method to rally your congregation or voters around you. That's not what he chose to do.

He stood up and said, "I know you're hurting. I'm hurting, too. We have every reason to hate our enemies as the death toll rises with each passing day. But that's not what Christians are called to do. We are called to love our enemies."

So often we hear about religion fanning the flames of hatred. Sometimes it does. Yet, I've watched it make people rise to the occasion and sacrifice their own interests in the name of peace, so often, that it's hard for me to see it that way. Not all of the people I discuss in this book are motivated by their faith, but many are. Whatever their motivation, these peacemakers are remarkable and their numbers are growing.

They exist on both sides. *History is made by people such as this.*

" ... we have been plunged into the abyss of oppression. And we decided to raise up only with the weapon of protest ... don't ever let anyone pull you so low as to hate them ... we stand in life at midnight ... always on the threshold of a new dawn ..." –Martin Luther King, Jr. during the Montgomery Bus Boycott (Zinn).

Activities. (2008) *Freedom Theatre*. Retrieved (Web. 2010, March 31) from http://www.the-freedomtheatre.org/activities.php

Alice Paul Institute (2008). Alice Paul: Feminist, Suffragist, and Political Strategist. Retrieved (Web. 2010, March 31) from http://alicepaul.org/alicepaul.htm

Anonymous Soldier. (2007). Personal interview.

Aramin, Bassam. (2007, Feb. 15). A Plea for Peace from a Bereaved Palestinian Father. *Common Ground News Service*. Retrieved (Web. 2010, March 31) from http://www.common-groundnews.org/article.php?id=20386&lan=en&sid=0&sp=0&isNew=1

Archives. *International Solidarity Movement Official Website*. Retrieved (Web. 2010, March 31) from http://palsolidarity.org/archives

Atkinson, Simon. (2006, April 10). British Peace Activist Was 'Intentionally Killed.' *The Guardian*. Retrieved (Web. 2009, April 2) from http://www.guardian.co.uk

Awad, Sami. (2008, March). Personal interview.

Bankier, David, ed. (2005). *The Jews are Coming Back: The Return of the Jews to Their Countries of Origin After WWII*. New York: Berghahn. Print.

Bannoura, Sa'ed. (2008, April 3). Troops Attack a Palestinian Family in Hebron. *International Mideast Media Center*. Retrieved (Web. 2010, March 31) from http://www.imemc.org/index.php?obj_id=53&story_id=57565

Bar-Tal, Daniel and Antebi Dikla. (1992). Siege Mentality in Israel. *Journal of Intercultural Relations* 16.3 Summer 1992: 95-7. Print.

B'Tselem. (2008, May 2). Archive. Retrieved (Web. 2010, March 31) from http://www.bt-selem.org/english/OTA

B'Tselem. (2008, May 2). Palestinians Who Died Following an Infringement of the Right to Medical Treatment in the West Bank. Retrieved (Web. 2010, March 31) from http://www.btselem.org/english/statistics/casualties_data.asp?Category=21&region=TER

Chacour, Elias. (2007, January). Personal interview.

Chacour, Elias, and Mary E. Jensen. (1992). *We Belong to the Land: The Story of a Palestinian Israeli Who Lives for Peace and Reconciliation*. New York: Harper Collins. Print.

Chacour, Elias, and Tom Weaver. (1984). *Blood Brothers*. Grand Rapids, MI: Chosen. Print.

Checkpoints. (2008, April 4). *Palestine Monitor*. Retrieved (Web. 2010, March 31) from http://palestinemonitor.org/spip/spip.php?article8

Christian Peacemaker Teams. (2008). Chronology. Retrieved (Web. 2010, March 31) from http://cpt.org/work/palestine

Christian Peacemaker Teams. (2008). News Archive. Retrieved (Web. 2010, March 31) from http://cpt.org/news/archives

Christian Peacemaker Teams. (2008). Projects. Retrieved (Web. 2010, March 31) from http://cpt.org/work/palestine

Combatants for Peace. (2007, January 7). Personal interview.

Corrie, Rachel. (2008). *Let Me Stand Alone: The Journals of Rachel Corrie*. New York: W.W. Norton. Print.

Courage to Refuse. (2008). Retrieved (Web. 2008, March 22) from http://www.seruv.org.il/english/movement.asp

Discriminatory Policies Against Palestinians in East J'lem. (2008, January 10). *Jerusalem Center for Women*. Retrieved (Web. 2010, March 31) from http://www.j-c-w.org/researchs.php

Elchanan, Rami. (2008). Personal interview.

Ellison, Joy. (2008, April 3). Archive. *I Saw It In Palestine*. Retrieved (Web. 2010, March 31) from http://inpalestine.blogspot.com

Fisher-Ilan, Allyn. (2007, June 27). Israeli Watchdog Calls to Lift West Bank Roadblocks. *Reuters*. Retrieved (Web. 2010, March 31) from http://alertnet.org/thenews/newsdesk/L27788364.htm

Flapan, Simha. (1987). *The Birth of Israel: Myths and Realities*. New York: Pantheon. Print.

Gish, Art. (2001). *Hebron Journal*. Scottdale, PA: Herald P. Print.

Golan, Neta. (2003, June 25). "The Long Journey from Nablus to Tel Aviv Writing from Nablus, Occupied Palestine." *Electronic Intifada*. Retrieved (Web. 2010, March 31) from http://electronicintifada.net/v2/diaries.shtml

Gregg, Richard B. (1966). *The Power of Nonviolence*. New York: Schocken. Print.

Hunsberger, Sally. (2007). Personal interview.

Irish Republican Army. (2007). *Info Please*. Retrieved (Web. 2010, March 31) from http://www.infoplease.com/ce6/history/A0825488.html

Israeli Bulldozer Kills American Woman. (2003, March 16). *USA Today*. Retrieved (Web. 2010, March 31) from http://www.usatoday.com/news/world/2003-03-16-american-woman-killed_x.htm

Israeli Committee Against Housing Demolitions. (2008). Frequently Asked Questions. Retrieved (Web. 2010, March 31) from http://icahd.org/eng/faq.asp?menu=9&submenu=1

Israeli Settlement. (2008, April 4). *Palestine Monitor*. Retrieved (Web. 2010, March 31) from http://palestinemonitor.org/spip/spip.php?article7

Izenberg, Dan. (2007, August 18). Bassam Aramin Says He is Waiting for Israeli Justice. *Jerusalem Post*. Global Exchange. Retrieved (Web. 2010, March 31) from http://globalexchange.org/countries/mideast/palestine/4916.html

Jarour, Maysaa. (2010, January 5). An Israeli Jewish Lives in Ramallah: This Country, Palestine, from the River to the Sea. *The Palestine Telegraph*. Retrieved (Web. 2010, March 31) from http://www.paltelegraph.com/diaries/85-diaries/3518-an-israeli-jewess-lives-in-ramallah-this-country-palestine-from-the-river-to-the-sea

Jefferson, Thomas. (2008). Notes on the State of Virginia 1784-5. *Project Gutenberg EBook of the Best of the World's Classics, Restricted to Prose, Vol. IX*. State U of New York. Retrieved (Web. 2010, March 31) from http://www.gutenberg.org/zipcat.php/28653/28653-h/28653-h.htm

Kamphoefner, Kathy. (2007). Personal interview.

Kapitan, Tomis. (2009, April 2). *International Ethics Page*. Northern Illinois U. Retrieved (Web. 2010, March 31) from www.niu.edu/phil/~kapitan/International%20Ethics.html

Khalidi, Walid. (2006). *All That Remains*. Beirut: Institute for Palestine Studies. Print.

Kurlansky, Mark. (2006). *Nonviolence Twenty-Five lessons from the History of a Dangerous Idea*. New York: Modern Library. Print.

Lennon, John. (1969). *Wedding Album*. Apple Records. LP.

Lerner, Eryan. (2007). Personal interview.

Mack, John E. (1990). The Psychodynamics of Victimization Among National Groups in Conflict. *The Psychodynamics of International Relationships, Volume I: Concepts and Theories*. Eds. Vamik D. Volkan, Demetrios A. Julius, and Joseph V. Montville. Toronto: Lexington. 125. Print.

Mar Elias Campus. (2008, March 2). *Nazareth Galilee Academic Institution*. Retrieved (Web. 2010, March 31) from http://mec.sahrat.net

Margolick, David. (2007, September 24). Through a Lens, Darkly. *Vanity Fair*. Retrieved (Web. 2010, March 31) from http://www.vanityfair.com/politics/features/2007/09/littlerock200709

Masalha, Nur-eldeen. (1992). *Expulsion of the Palestinians: The Concept of "Transfer" in Zionist Political Thought*. Washington DC: Institute for Palestine Studies. Print.

The Mennonite. (2008, March 31). Retrieved (Web. 2010, March 31) from http://www.themennonite.org

Myre, Greg. (2007, January 23). Father of Dead West Bank Girl Seeks Peace with Israelis. *New York Times*. Retrieved (Web. 2010, March 31) from http://www.nytimes.com/2007/01/23/world/middleeast/23mideast.html

News Archive. (2003, March 10). *Morning Edition*. NPR. Retrieved (Web. 2008, April 12) from http://www.npr.org/templates/story/story.php?storyId=1009

News. *Friends of Freedom and Justice - Bilin Official Website*. Retrieved (Web. 2010, March 31) from http://bilin-ffj.org/index.php?option=com_content&task=blogsection&id=1&Itemid=30

Ninety-Eight Percent of Gaza's Children Experience or Witness War Trauma. (2006, August 1). *Science Daily*. Retrieved (Web. 2010, March 31) from http://www.sciencedaily.com/releases/2006/08/060801183448.htm

Niva, Steve. (2003, March 17). Rachel Corrie, Nuha Sweidan and Israeli War Crimes. *Electronic Intifada*. Retrieved (Web. 2010, March 31) from http://electronicintifada.net/v2/article1250.shtml

Palestine News Network. (2008). Retrieved (Web. 2010, March 31) from http://english.pnn.ps/index.php?option=com_content&task=archivessection&id=o&itemid=45

Personal interview. (2008, January 4).

Personal interview. (2008, January).

Personal interview. (2008, June 24).

Personal Stories. (2008, April 6). *Parents Circle*. Retrieved (Web. 2010, March 31) from http://theparentscircle.com/stories.asp

Personal Stories. (2008) *Combatants for Peace.* Retrieved (Web. 2010, March 31) from http://www.combatantsforpeace.org/story.asp?lng=eng

Rahma, Abdullah Abu. (2008, February) Telephone interview.

Replacing Pain with Hope. (2008). *Parents Circle – Family Forums.* Retrieved (Web. 2010, March 31) from http://theparentscircle.com/stories/Rami_Elchanan.doc

Rishmawi, George. (2002, December 10). International Solidarity Movement. *ZNet.* Retrieved (Web. 2010, March 31) from http://zcommunications.org/international-solidarity-movement-by-george-rishmawi

Rosenberg, S. (2003). Victimhood. *Intractable Conflict Knowledge Base Project.* U of Colorado. Retrieved (Web. 2009, April 3271) from http://www.intractableconflict.org/m/victimhood.jsp

Rutledge, Gary. (2008, April 12). *Gary Rutledge Learning Site.* Retrieved (Web. 2008, April 12) from http://www.garyrutledge.com/AmHistory/hist_articles/1960s_articles.htm

Mission. (2008, April 3). *Shabbat Shalom: The Journal of Jewish-Christian Reconciliation.* Retrieved (Web. 2010, March 31) from http://shabbatshalom.info/article.php?id=17

Sharon Ready to Release Murderers if PA Lets Him Expel Jews Quietly. (2005, February 10). *Israeli Insider.* Retrieved (Web. 2010, March 31) from http://web.israelinsider.com/Articles/Diplomacy/4976.htm

Staub, Ervin. (1989). *The Roots of Evil: The Origins of Genocide and Other Group Violence.* New York: Cambridge UP. Print.

Testimonies. (2008). *Breaking the Silence.* Retrieved (Web. 2010, March 31) from http://www.shovrimshtika.org/testimonies_group_e.asp

The Trigger-Happy Phenomenon Continues. (2007, February 4). *B'Tselem.* Retrieved (Web. 2010, March 31) from http://btselem.org/English/Email_Update/20070204.htm

Weir, Alison. (2004, October 6). Heroism in the Holy Land: Chris Brown Beaten for Walking Children to School. *San Francisco Bay View.* Retrieved (Web. 2008, April 12) from http://www.sfbayview.com/2004

Wink, Walter. (1993, November 14). The Third Way. *30 Good Minutes.* Chicago Evening Sunday Club. Retrieved (Web. 2010, March 31) from http://www.csec.org/csec/sermon/wink_3707.htm

Woolley, John T., and Gerhard Peters. (1999). Dwight D. Eisenhower. *The American Presidency Project.* U of California Santa Barbara. Retrieved (Web. 2010, March 31) from http://www.presidency.ucsb.edu/ws/?pid=10232

Zinn, Howard. (1995). *A People's History of the United States.* New York: HarperCollins. Print.

CPSIA information can be obtained
at www.ICGtesting.com
Printed in the USA
FFOW03n0021230816
26996FF